# ■ PRAISE FOR *SUPERCHARGING SUPPLY CHAINS*

"More than a treatise, *Supercharging Supply Chains* gives senior managers clear, strategic insight linking this much-talked-about subject to free cash flow and shareholder value goals. Well organized, the authors provide a strong, practical framework for understanding how cost, time, and speed are changing the way successful companies achieve operational excellence . . ."

*—John W. Snow, Chairman, President,*
*and Chief Executive Officer, CSX Corporation*

". . . *Supercharging Supply Chains* is a book whose timing is right. In today's global markets, competition is fierce, and the best companies are competing more and more through operational excellence . . ."

*—Ken Watchmaker, Chief Financial Officer,*
*Reebok International, Ltd.*

". . . Probably one of the largest untapped opportunities in business today . . . *Supercharging Supply Chains* is loaded with practical advice on how to drive added value through integrated demand/supply management. We will put it to good use! . . ."

*—Ralph W. Drayer, Vice President, Efficient Consumer*
*Response, the Procter & Gamble Company*

". . . With this book, readers get innovative and strategic perspectives for the global and regional management of the entire supply chain. At the same time, large cost-reduction potentials are unlocked through supply chain management to improve your competitive position . . ."

*—Hans-Dieter Panzer, General Manager Logistics, Siemens AG*

". . . Supply chain excellence is being recognized as an integral part of designing and implementing successful business strategy and execution for profitable growth and increasing shareholder value. This book provides supply chain management executives with a valuable reference to respected thinking and timely business examples of what is important to consider keeping a company competitively at the forefront. Well done!"

*—Nicholas J. LaHowchic, President and Chief Executive*
*Officer, Limited Distribution Services, Inc.*

". . . *Supercharging Supply Chains* combines useful methods, impressive new approaches, and insightful business examples to think about the value of operations. Let me recommend this book as a weapon for any senior executive fighting in the global market."

—Dr. F. Hermann Krog, Corporate Executive
Director of Logistics, Volkswagen Group

". . . By starting with a shareholder value creation perspective, this book provides a crucial Rosetta Stone business rationalization for the supply chain. This business value context is critical yet missing in most other treatments of this material . . ."

—Bud Mathaisel, Chief Information Officer and
Executive Director, Ford Motor Company

"An insightful look into the reality of today's business challenges for both the logistician and business person. Read it. Believe it. Live it."

—Peter Peck, Vice President of Channel
Operations, Xerox Corporation

". . . The key to globalization is optimizing all of your resources world-wide, not just selling your product in 20 or more countries. Supply chain management, enabled by the right information technology, is fundamental to this goal. This book will be a valuable asset to all readers . . ."

—Thomas Trainer, Chief Information Officer, Eli Lilly and Company

". . . In times of global competition, an integrative supply chain approach is a key lever for offering outstanding value to the customer. If you want to learn about linking high-level business metrics (e.g., shareholder value or Economic Value Added) and operational excellence through modern supply chain management, this is the book to read."

—Klaus Goertz, Chief Executive Officer,
Hoechst Procurement International

"Very timely! For the senior executive who wants to maximize the Economic Value Added of his operations and the supply chains they partner in."

—Pat Guerra, Vice President, Corporate Supply Management, AMD

"*Supercharging Supply Chains* is a must-read for those seriously interested in value creation and for all students of velocity."

—Tom Meredith, Senior Vice President
and CFO, Dell Computer Corporation

# Supercharging Supply Chains

## NEW WAYS TO INCREASE VALUE
## THROUGH GLOBAL OPERATIONAL EXCELLENCE

Gene Tyndall
Christopher Gopal
Wolfgang Partsch
John Kamauff

*John Wiley & Sons, Inc.*

New York ➤ Chichester ➤ Weinheim ➤ Brisbane ➤ Singapore ➤ Toronto

Copyright © 1998 by Gene Tyndall, Christopher Gopal, Wolfgang Partsch, and John Kamauff. All rights reserved.
Published simultaneously in Canada.
Published by John Wiley & Sons, Inc.

**Library of Congress Cataloging-in-Publication Data**

Supercharging supply chains: New ways to increase value
   through global operational excellence / Gene Tyndall . . .
   [et al.].
       p.      cm.
   Includes bibliographical references and index.
   ISDN 0-471-25437-1 (alk. paper)
   1. Business logistics.   I. Tyndall, Gene R.
HD38.5.G583   1998
658.5—dc21                                      98-12034
                                                    CIP

Printed in the United States of America.
10 9 8 7 6

# Contents

# Acknowledgments

Developing a book with innovative content and practical ideas is a significant challenge even when time is available. However, as senior consultants and line partners in a leading global professional services firm, we have found repeatedly that there is *never enough time available*. Therefore, we thank heartily the many people whose energy, commitment, insights, and time helped move this book from concept to reality.

First and foremost, we extend our gratitude to the many client executives with whom we have worked in our combined 100 years of management consulting. Day-to-day, year-to-year, and engagement-to-engagement, we are reminded that consultants glean as much knowledge from their clients as they do from us. Because they are too numerous to cite individually, we can only hope that our many good friends and contacts recognize the ideas and concepts that they often encouraged us to document. To each of you, the four of us acknowledge and appreciate the relationships we have shared.

Second, we thank our editor, Christopher Roy, whose technical and journalistic competence gave this book additional power and reader-friendliness. We also appreciate his ability to clarify ideas and to facilitate and resolve the inevitable differences of opinion that accompany a group-authoring endeavor.

Next, we are grateful in many ways to our firm, Ernst & Young, whose blanket emphasis on clear, value-based solutions represents the ideological center of this book. We also appreciate the efforts of the core members of E&Y's Supply Chain Practice, and particularly the encouragement of three senior partners in our Global Management Consulting Leadership: Roger Nelson, Antonio Schnieder, and Terry Ozan. Throughout the firm, in fact, colleagues from many practices contributed a variety of ideas and stimulated fruitful discussion—all of which helped to make this a better and more useful book.

We acknowledge a special thanks to Gerry Marsh, Principal, High-Tech Analyst Group, for his substantial contributions to our shareholder value discussions. Gerry's knowledge and insight into true enterprise value and free cash flow have been especially meaningful to our strategic framework for operational excellence.

Individually, we thank Diane Rosenberg, without whose support this project would not have been possible. We are also grateful to Cheryl Buller, whose computer skills first put our words and ideas on the printed page, and to Barbara Quinn, whose artistic talents brought greater value and readability to the book's many graphics.

Last but not least, we would like to thank the publishing team at John Wiley & Sons, particularly business editor Jeanne Glasser and her staff, all of whom helped make this project a reality.

# Introduction

This is a book about operational excellence. It does not focus on a particular industry. It does not promote a particular business strategy. And it does not advocate the layoff of thousands or the spending of millions. Rather, it is simply a collection of common-sense, well-supported ideas . . . the kind that business leaders might collect on their own, *if* their schedules could accommodate more than a sporadic glimpse into operations, and *if* the connections between strategy and execution were much clearer than they often are.

The reality, however, is that most senior executives must be content with snapshot views of how their companies are performing. This is because most of their time needs to be spent developing and managing the strategic agenda—that is, *charting* the company's course rather than *steering* it. This is as it should be. Nothing is more important in the global economy than building the strategies and programs that frame superior, sustainable performance.

However, even if strategic leadership wasn't the senior executive's key job, other priorities might still sneak in ahead of operations. This is because a belief exists at most companies that significant inefficiencies have been purged from their systems, and that further economies would be subject to the Law of Diminishing Returns. Second, the

Gospel du Jour states that the road to competitive advantage and market leadership now runs through The Land of Increased Sales.

To an extent, we know these beliefs are true. Today, far fewer companies are bloated or inefficient. And in today's hypercompetitive world, significant increases in shareholder value *do* require a stronger focus on sales, marketing, and share. Nevertheless, operational excellence remains a greater imperative than most companies and most executives acknowledge. In fact, it is our contention that operational excellence is an essential—if not *the* essential—component of increased shareholder value. This is because operational excellence is *not* synonymous with efficiency. Operations refers to how the company organizes and practices the "business of business." So operational excellence really means, among other things, how well the company *actualizes* new products, new markets, new channels, and new competitive strategies.

If this were not true—that is, if peak efficiency were all that was required of operations—then far fewer of today's executives would be dissatisfied with their companies' performance. But this is far from the case, in spite of the decade's strong global economy. After all, numerous companies seem to have good strategies, sound financial goals, and an enviable acquisition record. Yet they consistently underperform operationally, and consequently, they are undervalued.

Thomas Alva Edison once said, "Genius is one percent inspiration and 99 percent perspiration." Our point is that operations is the perspiration: the actualization of good ideas . . . the *doing* that complements the *thinking*. That is why this book is about operational excellence. Because new ways to think about what your business *does* are as important as new ways of thinking about your business. Great ideas— made real by superior performance—are the key to beating the competition.

## ■ WHY WE WROTE THIS BOOK AND WHY YOU SHOULD READ IT

However narrow the perspective, it is likely that Wall Street will always place excessive weight on short-term performance ratios. It's a fact of business life. However, we believe that more and more smart money will flow ultimately to the stocks of companies that are exceptionally well operated. As explained in Chapter 1, this trend will continue because free cash flow is among the most important determinants of profitability. In turn, free cash flow is primarily a function of operations and working capital efficiency: the lower the capital or operating expenditure per revenue dollar, the greater the free cash flow and the higher a company's market capitalization. This is why operational excellence and supply chain management will, over time, become more and more respected as serious drivers of shareholder value.

The subsequent chapters of this book look at the many ways in which supply chain management can help companies enhance marketplace performance and, thus, shareholder value. Like any initiative, they are predicated on solid strategies, sustained commitment, and changes in attitude, culture, and organization. Most important, though, these ideas require more than senior-level buy-in or support. They require senior-level *involvement*. As a new key to shareholder value, operational excellence is too vital to be left to middle managers, who must continually justify requests for investment in operational improvements. Operations is the bridge connecting business strategy and shareholder value. Like never before, it must be crossed regularly by a company's most senior people.

Second, this book is a response to the requests we receive regularly from clients for a book-length collection of supply chain insights, "gems," and ideas. Taken together, our observations have helped to fuel a great many client success stories. Not surprisingly, other insights resulted from simply making mistakes. An obvious no-brainer, however, is that our senior-level friends and contacts are busier than ever and that their time is more fragmented. Thus, we are exceptionally pleased that they have requested our input, and we are pleased to oblige them.

Last, we recognize that the time to scrutinize operations does not magically appear simply because someone writes a good book on the relationship between operations and shareholder value. This is why we have tried to present our material as a logically sequenced compendium of ideas: a book that can be picked up and read one chapter—or one section—at a time. We have also included an "Ask Your Managers" section at the end of each chapter, which we hope will provide you with a clearer, larger, and faster-developing snapshot of current operations, and a better sense of where opportunities reside within your company. A wide variety of mini–case examples are also presented to prove, among other things, that there are endless ways in which imaginative companies can put good ideas to work. In these studies, we have revealed nothing proprietary. After all, our clients didn't hire us to publicize their secrets, innovations, or sources of competitive advantage. All of our "caselets" are available through public sources and are cited as such. The real innovation, concepts, and potential for unique competitive advantage are embodied in the context of the book.

We want this volume to be a "briefcase" book that is *marked up and used,* rather than displayed on a bookshelf. Every chapter (and most sections) of this book contain *useable* information on the value of operations: the things your company does every day and must continuously do better to succeed in a furiously competitive marketplace. Therefore, it is by design that reading this book will not make you an expert in supply chain management or operations—that would require a larger serving of minutia than would be appropriate here. Instead, the book's overriding purpose is to introduce and explain a variety of operational innovations that can help you work better and more productively with your company's supply chain leaders. Working together (with the help of this book), you and your staff will succeed in leveraging operational excellence to improve your company's shareholder value.

## ■ AN OVERVIEW OF THIS BOOK

Supply chain management is better understood than ever before. However, with increasingly global pressures, competition, and customer demands, new and broader supply chain objectives appear regularly. These objectives are business-unit wide and cross-functional. Often, in fact, supply chain initiatives are enterprise wide. They cannot be attached to holding departments or functions that are accountable for internal results. Cost, time (speed), and value-added services associated with products and channels provide the new rules of competition. The supply chain governs all three—and contributes to business growth.

Nevertheless, the basic supply chain paradigm remains an effective way to present new issues, goals, priorities, and concerns. This is why our book is presented in a comfortable *plan-buy-develop-make-move-sell* format. What's different is not the structure, but the ideas and activities that take place within it.

➤ Chapter 1 explains why increased shareholder/enterprise value is an increasingly direct result of supply chain excellence.

➤ Chapter 2 completes the connection by focusing on the supply chain characteristics that enhance shareholder/enterprise value.

➤ Chapter 3 kicks off the supply chain process with some nontraditional ways to think about and implement demand and supply planning.

➤ Chapter 4 presents new ideas about how and why operational (e.g., supply chain) excellence helps companies sell more goods.

➤ Chapter 5 introduces strategic sourcing and supplier management: an enterprise-wide approach to buying smarter and leveraging the value of procurement relationships.

➤ Chapter 6 examines the "new logistics": the untapped *marketplace power* of traditional distribution and transportation processes.

➤ Chapter 7 focuses on new product introduction and the critical (and underexamined) role that supply chain management plays in the lifelong health and marketplace viability of new products.

➤ Chapter 8 looks at what it all means: how the integrated, high-performance supply chain marshals and leverages all its resources to bring tangible, sustainable benefits to a company's bottom line.

Taken together, these chapters convey what senior executives need to know about operational excellence, and why they need to know it. As noted earlier, this is not the same as what a director of transportation, warehouse manager, or procurement specialist needs to know. It is what *senior executives* must understand about how the operating resources within their companies can best be deployed to maximize value. The point is: New ideas about how to handle regular business operations can help you differentiate your company in the marketplace.

Based on our many years of experience working with multinational companies, we are confident that the ideas in this book are fresh and useful, and that its most central tenet—that the achievement of supply chain excellence will reward its attainers with sustained enterprise-wide value—will serve executives well for a long time.

## THE IMPORTANCE OF GLOBALIZATION

Today, "going global" continues to be more of a goal than a reality. In fact, only a few companies have truly global brands, the right blend of centralized planning and decentralized decision making, and worldwide common processes and information technologies. Even fewer companies have found enough senior people with sufficient competence in global operations and logistics.

Nevertheless, "going global" is fundamentally a logistical undertaking. But it is not synonymous with selling or sourcing overseas or with becoming a successful importer/exporter. Instead, it is the highly coordinated international flow of goods, information, cash, and work processes. So "globalistics" is simply the leveraging of logistical (supply chain) excellence to enable this worldwide flow of the key components that make business work. Going even further, it is the marriage of traditional logistics (buy–make–move) with sales, marketing, financial management, and innovative partnering strategies.

So, although this book is not about manufacturing in Mexico, selling in Siberia, or transporting through Turkey, it *is* about the operating mechanisms that allow global companies to succeed.

# Shareholder Value: Is It the Business of Operations?

Want to increase your company's stock price? Perhaps bring the options above water? Regardless of whether a stock is market undervalued, analyses of more than 100 companies in several industries show that the effective management of assets improves *free cash flows* and, hence, true stock valuation.[1]

Consider that several drivers exist for determining and increasing a company's value. Revenue growth rate, operating income margin, effective tax rate, and working and fixed capital investment rates are among the most obvious. In the final analysis, however, *true stock value emanates from capital efficiency improvements.* Growth, in other words, must be profitable to be of value. How profitable? Profitable enough to generate healthy free cash flows: the money left over after subtracting expenses, taxes, and capital investment from revenues. And free cash flows (after taxes) only come from operations.

Certain companies clearly understand the intrinsic value of managing their working capital investment rate (defined here as accounts receivable–trade plus inventory minus accounts payable–trade divided by four times quarterly revenue). Compaq Computer, for example, consumes about 10¢ in working capital per revenue dollar, whereas Dell Computer uses a remarkably low 1.5¢ in working capital per revenue dollar.

Now compare these capital consumption figures with a number of well-known consumer products manufacturers that consume about 28¢ in working capital per dollar of revenue. Clearly, working capital efficiency has an enormous impact on free cash flow. The lower the capital or operating expenditure per revenue dollar, the greater the free cash flow and the higher a company's market capitalization.

---
*"Growth must be profitable to be of value."*

---

It is true that financial analysts apply simple valuation models such as price/earnings and earnings per share (EPS) to compare stocks and arrive at fair market values. But we also know that analysts' quarterly ritual for EPS guidance reinforces management's preoccupation with the quarterly income statement. The balance sheet, which reflects the capital efficiency side of the business, usually gets short shrift from sell-side analysts and management. However, it is the balance sheet that reveals both fixed capital efficiency as well as working capital efficiency—through metrics such as fixed asset turnover, accounts receivable days-of-sales-outstanding (DSO), inventory turns, and accounts payable days-of-purchases-outstanding (DPO). Managing these is the business of operations.

The longer the DSO, for example, the more money a company has tied up in assets for which customers have not yet paid, and the less money it has in free cash flow. One major manufacturer pays its suppliers in 15 days but does not collect from its customers for 90 days. As a result, this company requires additional working capital investment, suffers a lower free cash flow, and will probably experience reduced market capitalization as a consequence. The solution is not for the firm to lean on its suppliers by slowing down payments—although the corporation may have some latitude in that respect—but rather to fix the relevant business process(es).

Our analyses of more than 100 companies show that an untapped 20 percent of market capitalization could reside in the balance sheet: within those areas of operational excellence (such as inventory turns and DSO) that determine capital efficiency and free cash flows. Recent data show that a growing number of senior executives are beginning to understand that, at one level, expectations about future cash flow drive stock valuation. Are a company's production costs likely to go up? Can management gain market share? Is inventory growing excessively? These and other factors are good indicators of future cash flow.

> "*It is the balance sheet that reveals both fixed capital efficiency as well as working capital efficiency.*"

On an operational level, senior executives are also distinguishing between cost drivers that are influenced largely by external factors (e.g., markets and competitors) and those that are determined by internal, operational factors. The latter lie within their control. Recognizing this fact, senior management can identify and implement a portfolio of high-impact operational improvements that are free cash flow–based.

Those executives who understand that a company must earn more than its cost of capital before it can create shareholder value have an advantage over those who do not. Some of these executives have adopted financial statement–based ratios (such as return on capital employed) or economic measures (such as Stern Stewart's Economic Value Added, or EVA$^{sm}$) as key corporate performance indicators. These insights are major steps in the right direction. They indicate a true understanding that the balance sheet (and operational excellence) matter. Some companies go so far as to link balance sheet performance directly to executive compensation.

> *"A company must earn more than its cost of capital*
> *before it can create shareholder value."*

Although financial statement ratios and economic performance indicators point management in the right direction, they do not translate directly into stock price. No immediate causal relationship exists between stock price and such ratios and indicators. At best, these indicators are linked to stock price through a loose statistical correlation. A more powerful approach links cash flows to operating variables, which makes it possible to calculate stock valuations directly from an operating executive's point of view. This methodology is patterned after the Bond Valuation Model, a mathematical equation that helps calculate what a bond is worth based on its future free cash flows—that is, the stream of regular interest payments and the return of the principal amount on maturity.

## ■ SHAREHOLDER VALUE IS THE BUSINESS OF OPERATIONS

The aforementioned approach makes stock valuation not only understandable, but also demonstrates its dependence on operations. The methodology is especially useful for identifying high-leverage improvement opportunities on a large scale—at the enterprise or business unit level.

Naturally, the greatest positive effect on stock price comes from implementing high-impact, operational improvement programs on an enterprise-wide basis. Structurally and significantly improving, say, inventory turns and DSO can have a material impact on stock valuation and market capitalization.

This approach provides a powerful analytical tool that incorporates the company's value drivers and captures their interrelationships. It is invaluable for helping top management analyze trade-off opportunities and develop a prioritized portfolio of operational improvements, ranked by their impact on stock valuation.

As it turns out, all cash flows are not created equal when it comes to boosting market capitalization. Cash flows generated by revenue enhancement and cost reduction are taxed, often heavily. However, cash flows created from greater capital efficiency—through supply chain improvements to higher inventory turns or lower DSO—are untaxed. This means that 100 percent of these freed-up cash flow dollars contribute to improved market capitalization.

## ■ A CASE EXAMPLE

We recently performed a shareholder value analysis of a well-known consumer products company. Using publicly available information, it was determined that the company requires about 28¢ in working capital investment per dollar of revenue. Figure 1.1 is a three-dimensional graph of the company's Working Capital Investment Plane™. Think of this plane as a contour map of the side of a hill. The shaded bands represent 2¢-per-dollar changes in the investment rate. The company's inventory runs at about 4.2 turns, and its accounts receivable run at about 75 DSO. Thus, its working capital investment rate is the intersection of 4.2 turns and 75 DSO on the surface of the plane. This intersection point is on the boundary in the top left corner of the graph.

Now move to the left and follow the parallel lines to the left vertical axis. This will put you at about 28¢ per dollar. The company can slide down this plane by pushing up turns and bringing down DSO. The boundary between the bands in the lower right corner represents the combination of stock turns and DSO that result in a 14¢-per-dollar investment rate (i.e., eight turns and 45 DSO).

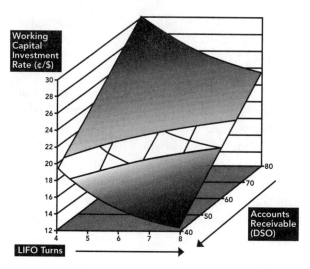

**Figure 1.1** The company's Working Capital
Investment Plane™.

It should be possible for this company to slim down to at least 14¢ per dollar of investment through operational excellence and the judicious use of commercially available information technology; however, such an initiative would require a significant commitment by executive management to be executed successfully. However, if the CEO doesn't focus on capital efficiency, *no one will*. It is a difficult undertaking that requires sustained effort and cross-company cooperation between the senior management team and their operating managers.

Next, Figure 1.2 plots the company's stock valuation against working capital investment rate. There would appear to be an opportunity to boost shareholder wealth by some 23 percent (more than $5 billion). However, it is important to remember that the slope of the line in Figure 1.2 is company specific. Also, the size of the stock valuation impact depends on the starting point. If working capital efficiency is bad—and 28¢ per dollar is not great—then the good news is that the company has a long and steep Working Capital Investment Plane to slide down. This translates to a big potential boost in market capitalization.

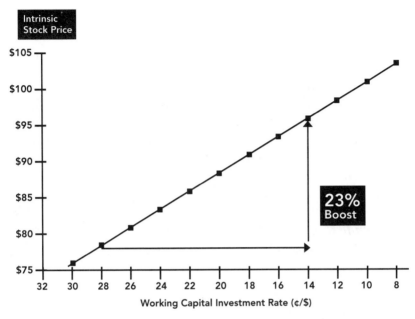

**Figure 1.2** The company's intrinsic stock price versus working capital investment rate.

## ■ THE GOAL

Operational excellence should not remain the purview of operations managers. It is both a competitive imperative and a shareholder value imperative. Boards need to ensure that the senior management team is capable not only of crafting a strategic vision and executing it, but also of focusing on and achieving operational excellence.

Like the aforementioned example, many well-known companies exhibit poor working capital efficiency and, conversely, face strong improvement opportunities and potential leaps in shareholder value. In fact, companies with much higher growth rates can expect much larger stock valuation impacts because of the compounding effect of revenue growth. This is due to the nonlinear relationship between stock valuation and revenue growth rate. If the revenue growth rate is increased by 5 percent, for example, stock valuation may increase 8 percent. This compounding growth explains the sky-high multiples on fast-growing, highly profitable companies like Cisco Systems and Microsoft.

There is substantial untapped opportunity, then, in virtually every company that has working capital investments that (as a percent of revenue dollars) are higher than its industry's leaders and the leading practice companies regardless of industry. As illustrated, their value proposition can be measured through a shareholder value analysis of publicly available information. This sets the improvement targets. Boosting a company's stock price in this way is certainly possible. *The challenge lies in management's hands, because operational excellence depends on a company's ability to optimize its supply chains.*

## ■ THE STRATEGY

The road to market leadership is paved with operating excellence and effectiveness, which, in turn, is the result of superior supply chain management: the making, buying, moving, and selling of a product.

What is supply chain management? By now, it is well understood by managers to be the coordinated flow of materials and products across the enterprise and with trading partners. But it also includes the management of information flow, cash flow, and process/work flows. Mastery (and integration) of these flows provides operational excellence (Figure 1.3).

The definition of supply chain management is well worn. But with increasingly global pressures, competition, and customer demands, new—and broader—supply chain objectives now exist. These objectives are business unit wide and cross-functional. And the supply chain initiatives to achieve them are enterprise wide. They cannot be attached to individual departments or focused internally. Cost, time

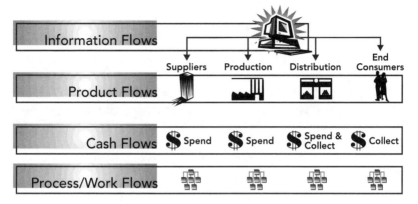

**Figure 1.3** Supply chain management flows.

(speed), and services associated with products and channels provide the new rules of competition. They are governed by the supply chain.

> "A supply chain is truly optimized when fairly priced products and exceptional services create unassailable levels of customer attachment and customer value."

As a general rule, companies with high-performing supply chains (Compaq, Dell Computer, Procter & Gamble, Wal-Mart, and Becton-Dickinson, to name a few) do have high-performing stocks. These companies work continuously to address five value drivers. Figure 1.4 identifies these drivers and notes the accompanying initiatives leaders often use to pursue them.

In practice, numerous strategies and performance measures can be adopted to move the business toward optimized supply chains. We believe a supply chain is truly optimized only when:

➤ "Bundles" of well-priced products and exceptional service create unassailable levels of "customer attachment" (acquisition and retention).

## PRINCIPLES FOR SUPPLY CHAIN EXCELLENCE

Supply chain excellence requires effective strategies, sustained management commitment, and changes in attitude, culture, and organization. Most important, however, it requires superior execution. As a guide to realizing this corporate state of being, consider the following "Principles for Supply Chain Excellence." These points are the basis of many of the more detailed success recipes offered throughout this book.

➤ Formulate a differentiated supply chain strategy by channel. For product categories, product channels, and target customers, develop an operating strategy that, when executed, makes your supply chain different from the rest. Focus on long- *and* short-term profitability, liquidity, and growth—all at the same time.

➤ Organize your business unit around major processes or channels, not functions. The supply chain is more than organizational functions, departments, or other traditional "silos," which separate work and interrupt flows.

➤ Work collaboratively with customers, suppliers, trading partners, and third parties to change the way operations are viewed, performed, and measured. Manage across the business on behalf of the customer. Think in terms of the *extended supply chain.*

➤ Invest or reinvest in supply chain information technology to manage flows end-to-end. Update your information systems and acquire packages that support both the planning and execution of the supply chain. Such systems include decision support tools that help decide what, when, where, and how much to buy, make, move, sell, and then measure results.

➤ Invest or reinvest in supply chain knowledge, people, skills, and learning. No person, team, process, or company ever knows enough or is aware of all the relevant leadership practices that could make a difference. Change is a constant, with innovations and problems always occurring. Organiza-

*(Continued)*

tions must invest in ongoing training, mentoring, education, and feedback systems.

➤ Operate or manage by product/channel. Think in terms of product-service "bundles" that are sold through channels, with each channel being different in terms of competitive needs. Supply chains should be set up and driven by the characteristics of the channels.

➤ Outsource elements of the chain for flexibility, higher performance, and better asset management. In many cases, the operating functions of the supply chain can be performed better by third parties. Management time should be spent on integration and innovations (new ways to excel), not on managing the transactions.

➤ Think globally . . . build regionally . . . operate locally. The best performing supply chains are managed with centralized planning, regional approaches, and local operations. Companies must design the right combination of these three elements, and then manage them better than their competitors.

Finally, *execute!* Focus on it, measure it daily (or in real time), and give people the authority and responsibility to excel at it.

➤ *Total* supply chain costs are at the lowest levels possible to ensure customer attachment.

➤ The supply chain contributes to profitable sales growth by creating and extending cost and service advantages, and by seamlessly introducing new products and phasing out old ones.

➤ Worldwide effective tax rates are at the lowest levels possible.

➤ Capital efficiency, working and fixed, is at the lowest level possible to ensure customer attachment.

➤ The supply chain is made flexible to respond to changes faster than competitors and to stratify service levels by product, customer, and geographical segment.

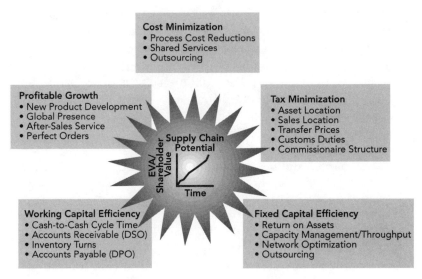

**Figure 1.4** The drivers of market value.

Obviously, these objectives and criteria represent ideal and absolute goals, reached in many areas by only a few of the best global companies. Still, tangible progress toward any of these translates into positive results, and shareholder value is impacted by every one.

> *"Improving the efficiency of the supply chain often requires structural or other changes that affect a company's tax burden. Only when the two are optimized together is shareholder value truly maximized."*

It should be noted that worldwide tax minimization, an area not integrated normally with business operations, has taken on new relevance with globalization and other supply chain influences. Improving the efficiency of the supply chain often requires structural or other changes that affect a company's tax burden. Companies that proactively consider the tax implications of those changes can significantly enhance the benefits of an optimized supply chain. Conversely, if the tax issues associated with any changes made to the supply chain are not addressed proactively, or if they are not addressed in the *current* structure, then these issues may erode the advantages gained by increasing the efficiency of the supply chain.

## ■ SEEK VALUE IN SUPPLY CHAIN OPERATIONS

More and more, improving the supply chain is seen as one of the best ways to improve the business. Although leading companies have always realized this, the time has now come for operational excellence and supply chain management to be recognized by senior executives in all industries as a true driver of shareholder value. Operational excellence, in the form of leading-edge supply chain management, has a

---

### ASK YOUR MANAGERS

1. Do your company's managers understand the role of operational excellence in creating value?

2. How does your company's operating performance compare with that of your competitors? Why? Do you really know if it is better or worse?

3. Do you know what value is present in the gaps between the best operational performance and yours?

4. Do you have programs or plans on the strategic agenda that address each of the five drivers of market value? Does this include tax minimization?

5. Do you have an enterprise-wide supply chain organization with managers accountable for operational excellence targets? Do you actually measure them in real time?

6. Do you focus on execution? What has been your performance *today?*

direct, positive effect on stock valuation. Top management, in other words, can turn great supply chains into greater shareholder value, because the business of operations *is* shareholder value.

## ■ ENDNOTE

[1]We credit Gerry Marsh, Principal, High-Tech Analyst Group, Saratoga, California, for his substantial contributions to this section. Gerry is a special consultant to Ernst & Young for shareholder value analyses.

*Chapter 2*

# The Business of Operations: Confronting the Issues

Chapter 1 established the connection between enterprise value and operational (supply chain) excellence. But what exactly *is* operational excellence? And how is it driven by supply chain management?

## ■ CHANGING MODELS: EXCELLENCE AS A FUNCTION OF VIRTUALITY AND TRANSPARENCY

To begin, we know that the operations of a business consist of several core activities:

- ➤ *Develop* (and design and introduce) new products.
- ➤ *Plan* for demand, supply, and inventory deployment.
- ➤ *Buy* materials and services.
- ➤ *Make* products.
- ➤ *Move, store, and deliver* materials and finished goods.

➤ *Sell* product, take orders, and provide customer services.

➤ *Market* everything.

➤ *Finance* the operations.

## ➤ Disconnected . . .

In most companies, the above core activities were historically detached. Each made its own semiautonomous contribution, which was measured and evaluated in an equally segregated fashion. Passing from function to function, products reached their destinations only after a series of handoffs. Nevertheless, in an environment of high margins, low customer sophistication, and minimal competition for the same marketspace, this "silo-oriented," production/engineering- (or marketing/sales-) driven model worked reasonably well.

## ➤ To Integrated . . .

Things are different today. More companies endorse (and many have adopted) an end-to-end "process" approach to business operations. Incented by information technology, stronger and more agile competition, price and margin pressures, and an increasingly demanding marketplace, most have abandoned management approaches that exclusively focus on growth or cost, separately managed functions, and internal performance metrics. In their place is a greater emphasis on profitable growth, liquidity, functional integration, communication, and (of course) the customer. With this enlightened view, they are positioned better to address differences among customer segments, geographies, and product lines. Also, unlike their silo days, they can balance customer management policies against the physical and financial realities of supply and demand.

## ➤ To Seamless and Transparent . . .

Many companies are also coming to depend more heavily on outsourcing and subcontracting relationships in one form or another. They understand that customers care about cost and service far more than they care about which specific entities actually sell, deliver, service (or, for that matter, *make*) products. So the key to satisfying those customers is *transparency:* a seamless supply chain that can address different customer segments in different geographies with different sets of products and services.

## ➤ To Virtual . . .

In the manifestation above—an integrated, multiorganizational supply chain—the key success benchmark is *market (shareholder) value.* Unfortunately, the key characteristics of today's marketplace—high fragmentation, more channels, and rapid proliferation of products and technologies—make the link between customer satisfaction and shareholder value very tenuous. Therefore, it should come as no surprise that "delighted" customers do not automatically produce delighted shareholders. On the other hand, flexibility, speed, liquidity, and cost are critical. Thus, competitive, market, and investor pressures are pushing many companies to a fourth operational stage: a highly *virtual* operational model populated largely by suppliers, third-party providers, subcontractors, and even customers. Figure 2.1 illustrates this progression of the supply chain organization: from traditionally disconnected, to more integrated, to seamless, and, finally, to the enterprise market value (EMV)–driven, virtual organization.

One of virtuality's key drivers (in addition to flexibility, cost, and a focus on core capabilities) is the idea that, beyond the synergies created through integration, all processes make a *measurable* contribution to business growth and profitability. With such a model, corporate structures can be focused on EMV, both as a tangible, desirable output and as a tool for managing the business.

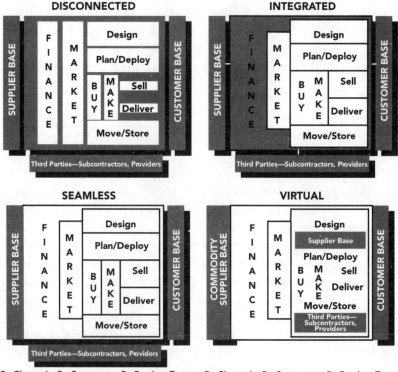

**Figure 2.1**  The traditional model of detached business functions has evolved into a more integrated business process model. This, in turn, leads to a seamless EMV-driven model characterized by segmented and focused operations. Now, more and more companies are moving to maximize EMV and flexibility by going to a virtual model.

## ■ MEASURING THE BUSINESS OF OPERATIONS

Companies work hard to measure detailed activities. But not many succeed at (or focus on) bringing a high-level dashboard view for senior executives to review and monitor. After all, senior executives are responsible for tying company activities to the three key metrics that define business success: EMV and share price, return on net assets, and net profit after tax. (In some situations, depending on financial position or market position, there is also an executive focus on revenue growth or liquidity—i.e., on the operating plan.)

---

*"One of virtuality's key drivers is the idea that, beyond the synergies created through integration, all processes make a measurable contribution to business growth and profitability."*

---

However, most business processes link performance with different measures: cost, response time, service, and to a lesser extent, information. And there is seldom any mechanism for associating them with "boardroom or business success metrics." The problem is that "process successes," such as improved customer service, sales growth, or attainment of cost reduction targets, can result easily in *lower* overall profitability, reduced flexibility, and unfocused capital investment.

*The challenge, then, is to develop performance measures at the functional level that track to the operating plan and boardroom metrics.* Figure 2.2 demonstrates this linkage between high-level, business success metrics and the supply chain. Making this connection operationally is worth the price of admission. It is what separates "focused activity" from "activity." As stated in Chapter 1, research has shown that stock price performance is linked closely to improved capital efficiency (working and fixed capital) and operational excellence (cost structure reduction, revenue growth, and tax minimization). *It is precisely these entities that are driven*

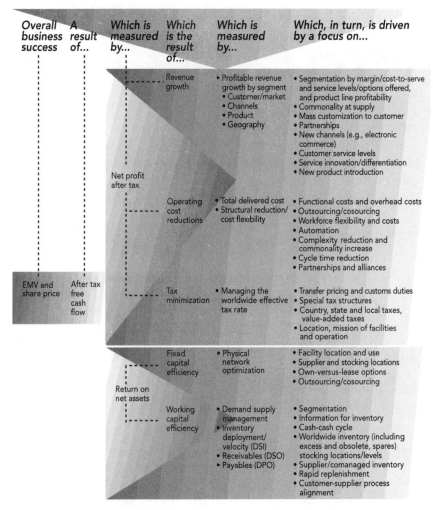

| Overall business success | A result of... | Which is measured by... | Which is the result of... | Which is measured by... | Which, in turn, is driven by a focus on... |
|---|---|---|---|---|---|
| | | Net profit after tax | Revenue growth | • Profitable revenue growth by segment<br>• Customer/market<br>• Channels<br>• Product<br>• Geography | • Segmentation by margin/cost-to-serve and service levels/options offered, and product line profitability<br>• Commonality at supply<br>• Mass customization to customer<br>• Partnerships<br>• New channels (e.g., electronic commerce)<br>• Customer service levels<br>• Service innovation/differentiation<br>• New product introduction |
| | | | Operating cost reductions | • Total delivered cost<br>• Structural reduction/ cost flexibility | • Functional costs and overhead costs<br>• Outsourcing/cosourcing<br>• Workforce flexibility and costs<br>• Automation<br>• Complexity reduction and commonality increase<br>• Cycle time reduction<br>• Partnerships and alliances |
| EMV and share price | After tax free cash flow | | Tax minimization | • Managing the worldwide effective tax rate | • Transfer pricing and customs duties<br>• Special tax structures<br>• Country, state and local taxes, value-added taxes<br>• Location, mission of facilities and operation |
| | | Return on net assets | Fixed capital efficiency | • Physical network optimization | • Facility location and use<br>• Supplier and stocking locations<br>• Own-versus-lease options<br>• Outsourcing/cosourcing |
| | | | Working capital efficiency | • Demand supply management<br>• Inventory deployment/ velocity (DSI)<br>• Receivables (DSO)<br>• Payables (DPO) | • Segmentation<br>• Information for inventory<br>• Cash-cash cycle<br>• Worldwide inventory (including excess and obsolete, spares) stocking locations/levels<br>• Supplier/comanaged inventory<br>• Rapid replenishment<br>• Customer-supplier process alignment |

**Figure 2.2** Enterprise Market Value consists of two pieces: net operating profit after tax (NOPAT) and capital allocations. Likewise, the supply chain function's principal mission is to increase the NOPAT and improve capital allocation. These relationships, their metrics, and the necessary focus to achieve them are described above.

*through the supply chain.* In fact, in most manufacturing companies, supply chain management is *the* key driver of competitive and market success. Therefore, it is vital—and possible—to translate functional performance measures to boardroom metrics and measure them continuously. This is the business model that should be tied to every company's success and compensation structure.

---

*"Process successes, such as improved customer service, sales growth, or attainment of cost reduction targets, can result easily in lower overall profitability, reduced flexibility, and unfocused capital investment."*

---

In net, each macro process—finance, market, design, and the supply chain—must be accountable for results that tie directly to business success metrics and shareholder value. This linkage of shareholder value to operations is what differentiates leading companies from those that are (or worse yet, *were*) merely good. After all, in today's business environment, being good is not enough. To please stockholders as well as customers, a company must be operationally excellent.

## ■ KEY BUSINESS ISSUES AND THEIR EVOLUTION

In the business world, there are three broad competitive requirements:

➤ Structure the organization for maximum flexibility and scope.

➤ Measure the right things, that is, those things directed at the success of the business.

➤ Frame a rapid response to the key business issues of today *and* tomorrow.

Affecting these three requirements are 12 key business imperatives whose future manifestations differ widely from those that we see today. These imperatives represent the supply chain management "ground rules" for tomorrow's companies. Executing them does not necessarily require heavy investment, but occasionally dramatic changes in management focus, style, and determination may be required . . . often in conjunction with some new managers.

The evolving issues presented in Figure 2.3 underlie each of these 12 imperatives.

---

**Margins:** Current margin pressures are severe. In the future, companies will manage margins differently, based on who buys what and who they deliver to.

| **Yesterday:** Sustainable margins | **Today:** Margin pressures | **Tomorrow:** Margin differences based on geographies, products, customer segments |
|---|---|---|

**Growth:** Today's growth levels track closely to geographical areas (e.g., Europe down, Asia up). These differences will become more acute in the future.

| **Yesterday:** Steady growth | **Today:** Growth differences by geography | **Tomorrow:** Accelerated growth differences by geography |
|---|---|---|

**Organization:** Many of tomorrow's leaders will be virtual companies: highly efficient managers of flexible alliances with multiple, changing business partners.

| **Yesterday:** Outsource noncore activities | **Today:** Virtual corporations, cosourcing | **Tomorrow:** Virtual corporations with a "consortium" approach to the market |
|---|---|---|

**People, skills, and compensation:** In the future, expect more segmentation of skill sets based upon geographies and cultures, as well as functions. Compensation trends show a new focus on value, such as tying stock options and bonuses to boardroom-level measures such as profitability.

**Figure 2.3** Key business issues and their evolution.

| Yesterday: | Today: | Tomorrow: |
|---|---|---|
| 1. Generalists | 1. Multifunctional | 1. Multifunctional/ multicultural |
| 2. Salary (pay for position) | 2. Salary/bonus (pay for performance) | 2. Salary, stock options, bonus (pay for loyalty, equity for performance) |

**Channels:** New channels are changing the nature of the game and opening the field, whereas existing channels are under pressure and undergoing change to retain market position.

| Yesterday: | Today: Direct: manu- | Tomorrow: Electronic |
|---|---|---|
| Control access to customer, middlemen provide service | facturers provide service and control access to customer; middlemen add services | commerce, new channels, anybody can play, consolidation of middlemen, customer ownership key, joint fulfillment ventures and specialized services, wide selection |

**Complexity:** More channels, globalization, customer types, products, competitors, and third-party options have made the supply chain very complex.

| Yesterday: One size fits all | Today: Movement to segmented supply chains | Tomorrow: Segmented supply chains, virtuality |
|---|---|---|

**Technology:** Technology is becoming part of the differentiation equation: from decision-support to communications to electronic commerce.

| Yesterday: MRP II/DRP systems automation | Today: Enterprise resource planning (ERP) systems with functional, decision–support add-ons; focused automation | Tomorrow: Best-of-breed, integrated decision-support systems; time to benefit, electronic buying, selling; Web-based technologies |
|---|---|---|

**Measurement and leadership:** Focuses on shareholder and enterprise value. Leadership is increasingly global with an emphasis on motivation and changing the rules of the game.

| Yesterday: Measure cost, variances; tenure is a qualification for leadership | Today: Measure processes and process outcomes; leadership linked to global focus | Tomorrow: Excellence measures tied to enterprise value; leadership dependent on focus, global motivation, changing the game |
|---|---|---|

**Figure 2.3** *(Continued).*

**Customer expectations:** Customer expectations are moving toward greater levels of service and response, with higher levels of customization.

| **Yesterday:** Product features and price dominate | **Today:** Service is part of the buying mix; growing demand for service | **Tomorrow:** More demand for customized products and services at best price (value) |

**Products:** Customers want less variety and more customization. Quality is an entitlement.

| **Yesterday:** Quality, latest features; internal development | **Today:** Lots of features; product proliferation; product/service bundles; joint supplier/ manufacturer development | **Tomorrow:** Mass customization with high-supply commonality; customized bundles: product/service/ customer/channel |

**Marketing:** Marketing will be much more focused to individual customers, with the supply chain expected to perform accordingly.

| **Yesterday:** Mass marketing | **Today:** Segmented marketing | **Tomorrow:** One-to-one marketing |

**Supply Chain Operations:** Supply chain operations will become increasingly alliance related.

| **Yesterday:** Competition among companies. One-to-one relationships | **Today:** Competition among supply chains (supplier, manufacturer, one-to-one, and one-to-many) | **Tomorrow:** "Co-option" between "grand alliance supply chains": supplier/ provider, manufacturer, channel partner, one-to-many, and many-to-many) |

**Figure 2.3** *(Continued).*

No company can excel in all of the supply chain imperatives. However, each must be part of an operational agenda and strategy. Therefore, the major operating tenet is "do less with more." This means focusing valuable resources on a few imperatives at a time, while maintaining parity in (or outsourcing) the others. Companies that can do this successfully will differentiate themselves strategically and operationally (Figure 2.4).

| THE ISSUES | THE RESPONSE |
|---|---|
| Margins | Global Operations |
| Growth | People and Training |
| Organization | Mass Customization and Postponement |
| People: Skills and Compensation | Operational Flexibility |
| Channels | Logistically Separate Operations |
| Complexity | Lean and Fast Supply Chain |
| Technology | Optimize Information |
| Measurement and Leadership | Customer/Product Segmentation |
| Customers (Expectations) | Collaborative Management/Virtuality |
| Products/Services (Bundles) | Electronic Commerce |
| Marketing | Operationalizing New Product Introduction |
| Supply Chain Operations | Dashboard, Cost, and Demand/Supply Matching |

**Figure 2.4** Responses to key issues define supply chain strategy.

## ➤ 1. Build in Flexibility

More and more, flexibility is the key to competitiveness—regardless of whether the company is asset-intensive (such as the semiconductor industry), has a high material cost content (like computers), or is distribution-dependent (such

### THE NEW IMPERATIVES OF SUPPLY CHAIN MANAGEMENT

1. Build in flexibility.

2. Plan and measure accurately.

3. Develop logistically separate operations where appropriate.

4. Get lean by emphasizing simplicity and speed.

5. Optimize information.

6. Treat customers unequally: segment and stratify.

7. Operate globally.

8. Practice virtuality and collaborative management.

9. Exploit electronic commerce.

10. Leverage people.

11. Operationalize new product introductions and phaseouts.

12. Mass-customize and postpone.

## OPERATIONAL INNOVATION: ORGANIZATIONAL STRUCTURE

**Becton Dickinson,** a global manufacturer of medical products, has created a new operating division called Becton Dickinson Supply Chain Services. The role of this unit is to integrate—and more effectively manage—all the company's supply chain processes and their interaction with BD's operating divisions. Becton Dickinson Supply Chain Services has forged a clear, competitive advantage for the company. Profitable growth, cost minimization, and capital efficiency are influenced every day by the best practices adhered to within this new division.

as in retail or consumer packaged goods). Regardless of the business, the ability to change quickly, efficiently, and effectively is essential.

In broad terms, flexibility has three tenets: *supply chain capacity, operations capability,* and *management's will to change.*

### Supply Chain Capacity

Supply chain capacity means flexible capacity and flexible cost structure, as opposed to fixed capacity and production inflexibility. For example, in several companies' operations, this entails the following:

➤ Deploying more temporary workers to complement a smaller, permanent workforce

➤ Investing in more flexible (and, sometimes, manual) production equipment that can be replaced, modified, and upgraded easily

➤ Considering smaller plants at different stages of production and geography, while postponing differentiation and order points as long as possible

➤ Using subcontractors, copacking, and outsourcing (everything from master suppliers to kit-and-assemble, to distribution and order taking, to production tasks typically done in-house)

Flexible capacity also has a time dimension. Airline pricing, for example, is based on capacity utilization—current *and* projected. Thus, pricing and quoted lead times are another way to attain flexibility in capacity. For example, longer quoted lead times to certain customer segments and for certain products—coupled with premiums charged for quick turnaround for other segments—are one way of providing capacity flexibility.

> *"Research has shown that stock price performance is closely linked to improved capital efficiency (working and fixed capital) and operational excellence (cost structure reduction, revenue growth, and tax minimization). It is precisely these entities that are driven through the supply chain."*

Additionally, flexibility is needed in the cost structure of operations. This is illustrated by the step function in Figure 2.5, which represents the traditional fixed-cost pattern used by many companies. Increasing flexibility means changing that pattern to more of a variable "straight-line" function that can be flexed in response to changing volume or demand. The goal is to reduce fixed-cost levels while leveraging those variable-cost components in which expenses can be reduced consistently or periodically. This is a key benefit of approaches such as outsourcing, joint partnerships, joint ventures, and cochannel management. Naturally, these strategies present greater difficulties for industries with very expensive production equipment (e.g., semiconductors). For them, a focus on pricing and lead-time quotes as a flexibility strategy is probably more appropriate. In many cases, the ability to ramp up or ramp down

### OPERATIONAL INNOVATION: FLEXIBILITY

**Lockheed Martin**'s Fort Worth, Texas, Air Force 4 plant has experienced substantial benefits from outsourcing and increased flexibility. Despite a 75 percent reduction in the volume of F-16s produced at the plant, Lockheed has cut production costs by 38 percent. One of the key contributors to this success was increased flexibility, enabled by such changes as the reduction of job classifications from 299 to 97. Another key factor was the outsourcing of more than 11,000 of the plane's parts, including some computers, electrical items, and sheet metal components.[*,†,‡]

*Jeff Cole, Andy Pasztor, and Thomas E. Ricks, "The Sky, the Limit: Do Lean Times Mean Fighting Machines Will Be Built for Less?" *Wall Street Journal,* 18 November 1996.

†Jeff Cole, Andy Pasztor, and Thomas E. Ricks, "Lockheed, Boeing Face Test to Meet Pentagon's Goal on Joint Strike Fighter," *Wall Street Journal,* 18 November 1996.

‡Jeff Cole, Andy Pasztor, and Thomas E. Ricks, "A Frugal Plane at $30 Million," *Wall Street Journal,* 18 November 1996.

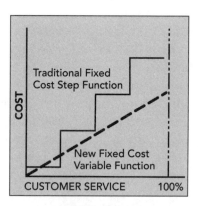

**Figure 2.5** Cost structure flexibility.

## OPERATIONAL INNOVATION: MASS CUSTOMIZATION

**Levi Strauss**'s Personal Pair Program allows consumers to custom-order jeans based on their exact measurements and desired color, material, and style. A computer-controlled machine cuts fabric to the jeans' specifications, tags it, and sends it through the standard manufacturing process. At the end of the production line, the tagged jeans are sent via FedEx to the consumer or to the store that placed the order.*

*http://www.startribune.com/digage/homshop.htm

more quickly and more effectively than the competition provides the greatest potential for sustainable competitive advantage.

> *"It is vital—and possible—to translate functional performance measures to boardroom metrics."*

Finally, flexible capacity means pushing things off your books onto someone else's . . . without relinquishing control. Good examples include supplier consignments and supplier

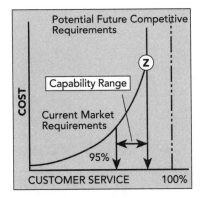

**Figure 2.6** Capability flexibility.

## OPERATIONAL INNOVATION: MASS CUSTOMIZATION

**American Express** is focusing on one-to-one marketing with its CustomExtras marketing program, which aims to treat the company's 30 million cardholders as individuals. The program, which uses a new data warehouse and other information technology, sends individualized messages and special offers to customers based on their exhibited spending behaviors.*

*John Foley, "Market of One—Ready, Aim, Sell!," *Information Week,* 17 February 1997.

management of certain corporate functions. For instance, some companies have suppliers manage their floor stock, tooling, and maintenance and repair operations (MRO) components. In turn, they may manage shelf space for preferred retail customers. Others have suppliers manage their outbound delivery, distribution, and replenishment; and the most flexible (and progressive) companies match their global capacity needs and levels to the tax and transfer pricing policies of specific countries or regions. By going beyond optimal site location and prudent asset management, they achieve operating flexibility and maximize their net operating profit after tax.

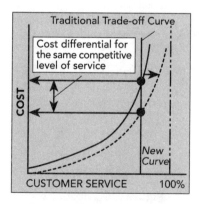

**Figure 2.7** Cost superiority.

### *Operational Capability*

Companies with flexible operational capabilities can deliver consistently high service levels ("Z" in Figure 2.6) within a superior cost structure. However, they also have the ability to *not do so* unless it becomes a competitive imperative. If the market, for instance, demands a 95 percent service level and the company has the capability to deliver 98 percent, it can either respond more rapidly than its competition when the market (inevitably) increases its expectations, or it can *create* the demand (and hence, the differentiation) by offering the higher service levels at the same cost. As shown in Figure 2.7, achieving such differentiation implies moving the classical cost/service trade-off curve to the right (providing better service for the same cost). This is done through innovation: changing the nature of supply chain operations in new and different ways. While competitors travel up (and down) the traditional industry trade-off curve (trading off costs and service along a narrow band), innovative companies define a *new* operational curve, providing higher levels of service at the same total cost. For example, a computer company should be able to configure and deliver a desktop unit in three days without sabotaging profit margin. But, in the absence of market or competitive pressures, it should also be able to configure (even more) profitably and deliver *over a longer period.* In other words, *no unnecessary excellence!* Unnecessary excellence highlights one of the major problems with classical benchmarking, which champions absolute levels of performance without considering competitive necessity or additional cost. Capability should be differentiated from day-to-day operational performance. They come together only when market or competitive pressures demand.

---

*"Flexible capacity means pushing things off your books onto someone else's."*

## Management's Will to Change and Adapt

"Will" is largely a corporate culture issue. It refers to the determination and ability (and executive management encouragement) of managers to experiment with everything from
contract manufacturing, to different supply chain constructs
(e.g., for new and existing customers and channel segments),
to new ways of doing business. This type of flexibility is a key
characteristic of leading, aggressive companies. For them,
calculated risk taking is often a barometer for supply chain
excellence.

## ➤ 2. Plan and Measure Accurately

Effective planning and measurement has three facets: a total-
cost approach to management, enterprise-wide demand/
supply planning, and a "dashboard" of select metrics to manage the supply chain.

---

### OPERATIONAL INNOVATION: PERFORMANCE MEASUREMENT

**Analog Devices,** a manufacturer of computer chips, has
worked hard to develop a "balanced scorecard." Once these
measurements, which contained nearly no traditional financial metrics, were put into action, senior managers began
meeting quarterly to discuss the results. When variations were
found from targeted measures, they were forced to address
what they would do about the variations. By 1996, Analog's revenues doubled to $1.2 billion from $538 million in 1991, and
operating profits rose from 3 percent to 19 percent.*

*Joel Kurtzman, "Is Your Company off Course? Now You Can Find out
Why," *Fortune* 135, no. 3 (Feb 17, 1997): 128–30. European, pp. 58–60.

---

### *Total-Cost Approach*

Companies must avoid management approaches built solely around visible segments of cost. For example, they must emphasize *total acquisition cost* rather than price-based procurement management and *total delivered cost* instead of manufacturing or distribution cost per unit. Over the longer term, this may require some sort of activity-based costing and management system. This is expensive and takes time. However, getting a handle on true costs can be achieved in much less time by working in a semiautomated mode on a periodic basis using financial operations analysts from the controller's group. More often than not, this approach is adequate for decision making. Moreover, many executives will have more confidence in the analysts' numbers anyway. In net, a total-cost approach helps determine true margins; establishes profitability by customer segment, channel, or product; and contributes to the evaluation of supply chain improvement and sourcing decisions (for example, whether to make a product or provide a service in-house or outsource it; and if so, to whom).

### *Demand/Supply Matching and Management*

Rather than depending on forecast accuracy and segregated demand/supply-planning processes, companies need to be *demand-driven and supply-aware*. This perspective must be accompanied by a focus on reducing operational cycle times to minimize the impact of the forecast. Although forecasting is important at a product group level (e.g., for capacity- and supply-planning purposes), it is far more effective to learn to respond quickly than to rely on an inherently inaccurate process for predicting demand. This is particularly true in industries where material costs make up the bulk of total product cost. Demand/supply matching and management must be enterprise wide and credentialized by senior staff.

This is the engine that drives costs and customer satisfaction, and it is crucial to operational excellence in today's complex, rapidly moving, and global environment. This topic is discussed in greater detail in Chapter 3. It is the key element in linking the supply chain, and it is this linkage that provides its strength.

| Operational Cost | Time and Response | Profitability and Margins | Customer Service |
|---|---|---|---|
| ➤ Total delivered cost by product | ➤ Total supply chain cycle time | ➤ Operational margins by product, channel, geography | ➤ Customer service levels by customer segment, channel, and geography along customer buying patterns and dimensions |
| ➤ Days sales/inventory (DSI) and levels | ➤ Order to customer (delivery cycle time) | ➤ Net operating profit after tax | |
| ➤ Excess and obsolete inventory | ➤ Response time to customer requests and orders | ➤ Effective tax rate | |
| ➤ Backlog and shortages | ➤ Postsales and service cycle time and time to fix | ➤ Return on total supply chain assets | ➤ "Perfect" orders |
| ➤ Days payable | | ➤ Cash flow metrics | ➤ Order-fill rates |
| ➤ Capital flexibility: fixed capital to total delivered cost | ➤ Supply P.O.: receipt time | | ➤ On-time delivery |
| ➤ Commodity costs to industry costs and trends | ➤ Manufacturing cycle time | | ➤ Delivery to customer request |
| ➤ Costs by channel, product line, and geography | | | ➤ Customer "convenience" measures |

**Figure 2.8** A dashboard must have a few, easily measurable metrics that monitor the pulse of the supply chain.

### *Dashboard*

The dashboard concept is crucial in operational measurement, monitoring, and management. Essentially, it refers to a few key metrics that define and measure the pulse of operations globally (like the dashboard in a car). In the best companies, these key metrics fit into four categories: operational cost, time and response, profitability and margins, and customer service (Figure 2.8). A good rule of thumb is to have no more than from five to seven metrics, with data collected and monitored in as near real time as possible. Too many companies use a measurement system that contains overly complicated metrics, contains too many metrics, or uses metrics for which reasonable data cannot be collected quickly. There are systems available today that provide such a dashboard ability for most of the key metrics at comparatively low cost, even in a complex supply chain environment. This is a very worthwhile investment when you consider how much money is spent on information technology in a typical company.

## ➤ 3. Develop Logistically Separate Operations

The optimal supply chain is precisely that: *a chain*. Interconnected links that work together. In many instances, supply chains (and segments of supply chains) that are excellent for one purpose (e.g., in a low-cost, high-efficiency, stable-product-technology, long-product-life cycle environment) will not be very effective for another (e.g., a rapid-product-life cycle, availability-driven scenario). Some companies focus erroneously on developing a one-size-fits-all supply chain approach that, by virtue of its singularity, is weaker and less flexible. This is the lowest-common-denominator supply chain. The point is that a single approach and set of capabilities can rarely optimize performance by every channel and customer segment. Where appropriate, companies need to emphasize *logistically separate operations* based on product and channel/market characteristics, and then consolidate expensive infrastructure wherever possible.

Consider for a moment the myriad entities that comprise the supply chain: suppliers, manufacturers, distributors, third-party warehousers, freight forwarders, contract carriers, third-party logistics partners, third-party maintenance companies, financing companies, and import/export brokers. Then layer in the order conduits that impact the process: fax, Internet, telephone, sales force, point-of-sale orders, EDI, and e-mail. Next note the growing number of fulfillment channels: direct-home, direct-business, retailers, value-added resellers, mass merchandisers, OEMs, service centers, and integrators. Finally, remember that processes must consider multiple customer segments, geographies, and product lines. This exercise should make it obvious that, end-to-end, any supply chain is enormously complex. Less evident, however, are the dangers posed by trying to manage it on a purely material-flow basis with a single model for every situation.

Figure 2.9 represents a classical-flow view of the integrated supply chain. Companies seeking to streamline the supply chain and maintain a low-cost/high-flexibility structure need an alternative to this method. They need to develop distinct management structures and approaches for channels, segments, and products: *logistically separate operations.*

Depending on the nature of the business, there are several approaches to developing logistically separate operations, and none are mutually exclusive. One is to segregate operations based on the characteristics of the traditional fulfillment and replenishment model:

➤ A *value-added process* (the traditional fulfillment model for products)

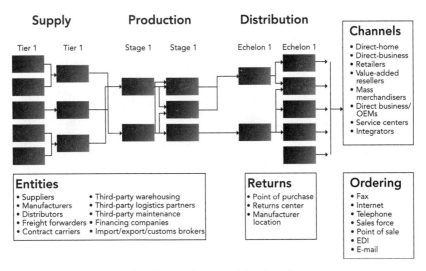

**Figure 2.9** The classical view of the fulfillment process: integrated supply chain management.

➤ *A service/repair process* (after-sales and reverse logistics: customer service, returns, repairs, warranty tracking)

Another approach is to set up discrete supply chain operations by type and nature of product. This implies differentiation according to:

➤ *Commodity product,* in which the major characteristics are managing working capital and cost structure. Here, efficiency is the watchword.

➤ *High-change product* (very short life cycles, high degree of alteration and innovation), in which the major characteristics are availability, new product phase-in/ phaseout, and a high degree of flexibility. Here, flexibility and response are the parameters.

A third approach is to set up discrete supply chain operations by channel, such as:

➤ *Large retail/mass merchandiser:* fulfillment and replenishment in the retail/mass merchandiser industry

➤ *Direct:* in which the company bypasses the middleman and goes direct to the customer

➤ *Fragmented retail:* supplying traditional small and "mom-and-pop" stores

➤ *Direct flowthrough:* in which the product does not physically touch the company's operations

A fourth perspective is to manage and structure supply chain(s) explicitly to handle products at different stages in their life cycles and adoption processes. Borrowing from Geoffrey Moore's *Inside the Tornado,*[1] alternative supply chain structures might include:

➤ *Bowling alley:* profitability management, product/service bundles, high flexibility

➤ *Tornado:* high availability and high volume

➤ *Main street:* low-cost, high-volume strategies with high-service bundles

This segregation is crucial because each strategy and channel necessitates different (and sometimes very significant) supply chain behaviors, including cost structures, core capabilities, investment and partnership methods, success measures, and management styles and approaches.

A key point to keep in mind, however, is that optimal fulfillment is not managed by a single supply chain or a single demand-management chain. Rather it is handled by two or three interlocking processes, each of which may be (and probably is) controlled by different companies. Examples of this are shown in Figure 2.10. In a retail environment, for example, the fulfillment process from the customer group is controlled by the customer (manufacturers do not control the actions of customers walking into the retail store). Like-

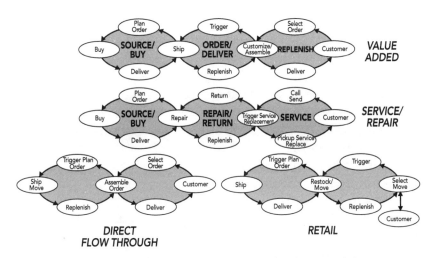

**Figure 2.10** Variations of the supply chain model.

wise, retail-level restocking, replenishing, and acquiring become the purview of the retailer; whereas planning, ordering, shipping, delivering, and restocking activities belong to the manufacturer. The key point is that *these activities are not one integrated process.* Each has different goals, margins, EMV targets, and market dynamics that make complete integration very difficult (if not impossible).

The danger with extended supply chains is their vulnerability during *handoffs.* Every intersect point between internal functions or external partners and suppliers represents an opportunity for money to slip through, information to deteriorate, costs to increase, and customer service to degrade. Every handoff (and there are many) is a chance to fumble the ball. Problems of all kinds congregate along the faultline: communication breakdowns, breaks in authority and ownership, inventory and material buildups, quality slips, and process inefficiencies. This is why *integration*—the management of linkages between supply chain partners—is crucial. Management efforts to improve the flow of information and material must focus on better handoffs among separately optimized supply chains.

## ➤ 4. Get Lean by Emphasizing Simplicity and Speed

Lean supply chain operations can reduce costs and increase flexibility. However, *getting* lean requires significant shifts in operational behavior. The most fundamental of these is *simplifying* product lines, part-numbering systems, communications, customer sets, and other aspects of the firm's operations; in other words, reducing complexity and increasing commonality in operations. The paybacks for simplification are enormous: improved capability, capacity, flexibility, consistency, and cost superiority, to name a few. Best of all, expensive information systems and other large investments typically are not required.

An often overlooked aspect of simplification is to reduce *uniqueness* (e.g., in parts, designs, suppliers, processes) and *variety* (e.g., of transportation resources, parts suppliers). Simplification can also mean establishing a common product language that extends from suppliers through design, manufacturing, marketing, sales, and the customer. Such a

---

### OPERATIONAL INNOVATION: LEANNESS

**Lantech,** a manufacturer of stretch-wrapping machines, adopted lean manufacturing concepts to reduce lead times and production costs. After standardization of work tasks and dramatic reductions in changeover times, the company was able to produce a machine in half the space it needed previously. Plus, the number of machines shipped doubled with no increase in the workforce. The order-to-ship cycle time of the company's most popular machine was reduced from 16 weeks to 14 hours. During the same period, Lantech's market share of the stretch-wrapping industry increased from 38 to 50 percent.*

*James P. Womack and Daniel T. Jones, "Beyond Toyota: How to Root Out Waste and Pursue Perfection," *Harvard Business Review,* September 19, 1996.

## OPERATIONAL INNOVATION: LEANNESS

**Motorola** improved factory logistics by replanning factory layout, work flow, material-handling processes, and material control. Results from the company's leanness initiative included smaller inventories, real-time information flow, short material pipelines, and orderly material handling. Some of the benefits were reduced cycle time and WIP inventory; improved customer service; improved accuracy of inventory (almost 100 percent); implementation of real-time, paperless inventory control; and expanded output and productivity.*

*James K. Allred, "New Direction," *IIE Solutions*, 28, no. 4 (April 1996): 21–5.

system should emphasize standardization in part numbering, coding and classification, and cross-referencing across companies.

The second fundamental shift is *increasing speed*. This means reducing cycle times and managing demand/supply and deployment to generate maximum *inventory velocity* of material. Put another way, companies need to ensure that as little product as possible sits still. Remember that in the classic cost/service trade-off curve, the higher the service level, the greater the cost. Many companies still manage to this paradigm. However, by managing velocity (the speed and direction of product), companies can improve customer service and reduce costs simultaneously! Trade-offs in the supply chain are not a given! Managing and improving velocity requires a combination of supply chain management disciplines, including inventory segmentation by product, channel, and geography, and enterprise-wide demand/supply matching and deployment. The glue is information (not information *systems*). Better and more readily available information accelerates product flow, making it easier to provide optimal service cost-effectively and stratified (no unnecessary excellence) levels of service that increase margins.

---

### OPERATIONAL INNOVATION: LEANNESS

**Jaguar** has adopted lean manufacturing techniques: building products only when they are needed, applying sensible levels of manufacturing technology, and reducing inventory at all levels in manufacturing. As a result, the company was able to produce twice as many vehicles using only half the people. The quality of the vehicles became significantly better as well. Quality, delivery performance, and unit cost reduction are some of the major benefits of leanness.*

*John Crampton, "Lean Manufacturing is Just a Start," *Interavia Business & Technology,* 51, no. 602 (August 1996): 24–5.

---

Although a lean supply chain may be simple to articulate, it is not simply a buzzword. "Leanness" requires discipline, common sense, and a great deal of management will and focus to implement. Beginning with the core concepts of simplicity, commonality, and speed, companies must work along multiple dimensions to:

➤ Reduce working capital employed (structurally, not just one-time) and increase liquidity.

➤ Reduce fixed capital employed (be more virtual by reducing bricks and mortar).

➤ Drive ownership, results, and focus, reduce number of accountabilities per key business result (preferably down to *one*).

➤ Establish a system of key, easily measurable dashboard metrics that monitor the operational pulse with real-time data. These data should be widely understandable, wholly measurable, and contain key executive accountabilities for each. Moreover, links should be established from the business metrics and EVA to the operational dashboard and compensation.

➤ Reduce churn for new products and designs, through part/module commonality and integration of design and development into demand/supply management and other processes.

➤ Reduce the number of exceptions to process (standardize as far as sensible and possible, globally).

➤ Emphasize and establish an enterprise-wide program of data ownership, accuracy, and integrity. Poor, inaccurate, or untimely data are the hidden reef that can sink an operation.

➤ Establish programs with suppliers, customers, trading partners, and service or asset providers to drive codecision making, coplanning, and execution for speed, effectiveness, and anticipation of market response. In other words, link processes with these members of the extended supply chain. For example, tie a key customer's ordering and buying process into the company's inventory, demand/supply, and distribution processes via information and joint planning.

➤ Do less with more . . . focus on fewer projects and corporate initiatives, and consider logistically separate operations.

## ➤ 5. Optimize Information

Many people confuse the need for information with the perceived need to buy and implement large information *systems*. Too often, these decisions are driven by senior financial or information officers who desire higher levels of standardization (e.g., for financial reporting, platforms, applications). Although large, global, enterprise-wide systems do provide these benefits when well implemented, they don't always improve the strategic management of operations or its execution at a tactical level, and they don't always provide them *quickly*.

The decision to install a major new system needs to have solid business drivers and a cost/benefit case behind it. Otherwise, the costs of disruption and lost opportunities can be too high. The key question is: How will this investment help us grow, cut costs, achieve flexibility, or increase competitive advantage? Also, companies need to assess the system's potential for connectivity with acquisitions, joint ventures, and trading partners. Consider following four aspects of supply chain systems acquisition and development.

### *Focus on "Time to Benefit" and Decision Support*

This is defined as the elapsed time between the decision to acquire a system and the time when it starts providing benefits. Given this definition, the key is emphasizing *process-based* and functional systems, such as demand/supply planning and optimization, rather than all-encompassing, "cover the enterprise" transaction systems. Nowadays, some large companies are spending huge amounts of money and resources on major transaction-oriented enterprise resource planning (ERP) systems. Because these systems also take years to install in a multioperation, multigeography environment, they must be justified in terms that go beyond "a need for improved technology." After all, by the time such systems are fully implemented, the technology may be somewhat obsolete. Worse yet, business conditions may have changed, thus rendering expensive functional features inappropriate for the current business environment. A final caution is that these giant one-size-fits-all systems are seldom perfect fits with every company's multiple channels and operations. Companies that think otherwise should expect many additional costs for "bolt-on" systems, modification, and redefining operations to implement the system. Some large-scale ERP systems vendors, however, are making significant effort to provide methods, tools, and templates to accelerate implementation, while adding supply chain modules and functionality as part of an integrated system. If the time to benefit can actually be reduced, adequate functionality can be provided, and the system and data are integrated without too much effort, this can be the best of all worlds.

An alternative approach is a smaller system with a process focus, decision-support capabilities, and a relatively quick implementation cycle. Because of the vendor's experience and expertise, these systems are likely to be functionally rich and sophisticated. Such an implementation could bring in major benefits faster and be upgraded or replaced relatively painlessly when new releases and technologies become available or when business needs change. The keys, as always, are to carefully define time-to-benefit and rigorously challenge value propositions and business cases.

Here is an even more radical approach to improving informational capabilities. Make users and managers responsible for key data. Increase their ability and authority to acquire smaller, targeted systems, which must be integrated into the overall information systems plan for standardization. Also increase their reporting flexibility and create new opportunities to customize analyses. The benefits of flexibility, speed, functional fit, and economy typically outweigh the traditional issues of integration and control.

### Take Ownership of Customer Information

Customer information has become far more than just the basis of how much product to make; instead, it is the driver for every key business decision. This is why tomorrow's leaders are those that do the best job of gathering, accessing, slicing, dicing, and leveraging customer information. For example, many companies currently capture point-of-sale (POS) data. However, fewer businesses leverage that data to predict buying patterns; assess channel options; and perform segmentation of customers, markets, or pricing structures. Information *about* the customer is the company's link *to* the customer. A good example is data mining, which focuses on the ability to develop "individual customer franchises" by isolating and assessing microcustomer buying, delivery, and preference patterns. Customer information, based on an understanding of intent, is the key: the real-time link to real-time order management and real-time demand and supply management.

Perhaps the most untapped value of information ownership is defining customer needs that have not been articulated by competitors or even by the customers themselves (in essence, uncovering latent demand). General Electric, Procter & Gamble, and Microsoft, for example, developed (and continue to create) customer needs and solutions where none existed previously. Before FedEx, nobody did much overnight delivery. Before Dell Computer, nobody thought of building computers to the customer's individual specifications. In both cases, a whole new channel resulted.

### Focus on Data

An elegant information system is quite useless (and probably harmful) without accurate data in which people have confidence. Operational capabilities will quickly break down without accurate data. This is why maximum emphasis should be placed on data ownership, data integrity, data accuracy, and data accessibility. Driven by executive staff, an ongoing data-quality program is needed within most companies. Once again, companies need to think less in terms of monolithic systems, and more in terms of integrating multiple systems with common data, or an integrated system with the functionality and built-in processes needed to help *manage the business.*

### *Replace Assets with Information*

Information systems create a worldwide union of suppliers, manufacturers, distributors, third parties, brokers, finance companies, customers, and consumers. In effect, they make possible a global supply chain that is more digital than physical. However, worldwide information assets do not necessarily imply the need for a single, common, worldwide architecture as a prerequisite. In fact, well-integrated, smaller systems—like multiple supply chains—can be equally or more effective. The key is timely, accurate exchange of common information (in a common format and standardized nomenclature) to increase flexibility, improve accuracy, control costs, and increase accountability.

The link here is inventory and the accuracy and timeliness of inventory data. Historically, inventory was moved and handled several times before reaching its final destination. Now the goal is to replace the physical movement of materials with digital movement of customer and product *information*. Instead of moving material and accumulating costs based on forecasts and some predicted use, a company initiates the physical flow only when an order arrives. So it moves inventory *once:* quickly and inexpensively.

## ➤ 6. Treat Customers Unequally: Segment and Stratify

Few companies practice "profitable customer management." Sometimes this is because their notion of superior service has no shades of gray (for example, a singular mission to "delight" all of the customers all of the time). Other times, it is because their operational model offers no insights into relative customer value. Whatever the reason, customers *are not* all equal and should not be served equally. Consider, for example, that the customers of a single company can occupy different markets, produce different margins, represent varying potential for growth, and engender a range of selling, administrative, and service or replenishment costs. Segmenting supply chain services based on these criteria is probably one of the most effective ways to improve EMV. Unless there is a strategic imperative, high (and expensive) levels of service provided to low-margin or nonstrategic customers can only damage profitability and divert resources from other areas. As mentioned earlier, companies must be able to provide excellent service to their most valuable (i.e., high-margin, strategic, high-volume) customers. But they must also offer a range of less costly services for those customers who are "less equal." One spin on segmented service exists in the airline industry, where price and service levels are based on capacity and availability. Another is practiced by manufacturers that price products based on varying lead times.

---

*"Companies' service approaches must be stratified according to the strategic and economic value of the customer and the cost involved in serving that customer."*

---

Simply put, companies' service approaches must be stratified according to the *strategic and economic value of the customer and the cost involved in serving that customer.* If a customer does not need product for ten days, there is no point in delivering it in eight days. The only payback for early arrival may be extra logistics costs for the manufacturer and added carrying costs and disrupted just-in-time (JIT) schedules for the customer. A relevant mantra is: *No unnecessary excellence.* Figure 2.11 illustrates some relative differences by customer segment in service levels for a particular company, which, of course, translate into differing costs to serve. The question that too many companies duck is: To which customer segments do we provide lower levels of service, and which do we stop serving? For instance, in the

| Mass Merchandisers (Total Sales: 350M) | | | | | |
|---|---|---|---|---|---|
| **Desktops ($1,100M)** | | **Notebooks ($400M)** | | **Servers ($200M)** | |
| Time to distribution center (DC) | 72 hours | Time to DC | 48 hours | | |
| Service level | 99% | Service level | 99% | | |
| Sales | $250M | Sales | $100M | | |
| Margin | 2% | Margin | 4% | | |

| Value-Added Resellers (Total Sales: 700M) | | | | | |
|---|---|---|---|---|---|
| **Desktops ($1,100M)** | | **Notebooks ($400M)** | | **Servers ($200M)** | |
| Time to Regional DC | 72 hours | Time to RDC | 72 hours | Time to RDC | 5 days |
| Service level | 92% | Service level | 95% | Service level | 95% |
| Sales | 450M | Sales | 50MM | Sales | 200M |
| Margin | 6% | Margin | 6% | Margin | 14% |

| Direct to Customers (Total Sales: 650M) | | | | | |
|---|---|---|---|---|---|
| **Desktops ($1,100M)** | | **Notebooks ($400M)** | | **Servers ($200M)** | |
| Delivery days | 5 | Delivery days | 5 | | |
| Service level | 95% | Service level | 95% | | |
| Sales | 400M | Sales | 250M | | |
| Margin | 10% | Margin | 12% | | |

**Figure 2.11** Sample customer service segmentation. Different customer segments and service levels have different requirements and different costs to serve.

hypothetical example shown in Figure 2.11, should we continue dealing with the mass merchandisers or, at least, serve them differently?

## ➤ 7. Operate Globally

Markets and customers are quickly, and enthusiastically, going global. Many companies, on the other hand, *consider* themselves global; but really, they are mired in a simple export-import mode. The point is, going global means a lot more than just selling products in other countries. Figure 2.12 describes the stages of going global, along with some of the supply chain characteristics that define the state.

Becoming an international or global player involves many special challenges, including standardizing business processes, nomenclatures, and data; sourcing and obtaining global materials; ensuring order and customer visibility; and managing different standards, platforms, and infrastructures. This is why

| Strategic Area | Export-Import | International | Global |
|---|---|---|---|
| Products | Domestic (U.S.)–produced and shipped | Market customization (items, packaging, etc.) | Global brands with common packaging |
| Markets | Variable | Across borders (two or more) | All four major regions of the world |
| Supply chain management strategies and operations | ➤ Ship/receive across borders using agents and distributors<br>➤ Volume-driven<br>➤ Transportation-driven<br>➤ Limited IT | ➤ Distributors<br>➤ Subsidiaries<br>➤ Some regional production/sourcing<br>➤ Decentralized management/operations<br>➤ Uncommon processes and IT | ➤ Global sourcing and distribution<br>➤ Centralized planning with regional/local executions<br>➤ Operations optimized globally/regionally<br>➤ SKU rationalization<br>➤ Common processes/IT integration<br>➤ Worldwide minimized taxes |

**Figure 2.12** The primary stages of going global . . . it's not automatic for everyone.

a single, global process, supply chain, or information system may not always be the answer.

Furthermore, global demand/supply management requires a new level of process and management expertise. For example, systems, procedures, and process information must be in multiple languages. Moreover, pan-European operations must still be segmented by infrastructures that vary widely, even within specific countries such as (unified) Germany. In countries like Mexico, relatively modern business practices may conflict with an inadequate infrastructure. And in India, channels may be defined by the way product moves to the retailer—by truck, by cart, or even by human.

International tax regulations provide yet another level of complexity. Locating a plant in Ireland, for example, versus elsewhere in Europe could mean several after-tax percentage points. In many geographies, global sourcing means trading lower costs for less flexibility—a lesson that many U.S. companies are learning in their domestic operations.

A final key point is that not every company *should* be completely global. Although most companies that operate across multiple geographies need centralized demand/supply planning with local and regional execution, not all need to pursue global sourcing, global manufacturing, global brands, and global packaging. When appropriate, however, operating in a global fashion can provide significant advantage in terms of sourcing, commonality, focus, cost, and flexibility in moving materials across geographies to capitalize on differing demand patterns.

## ➤ 8. Practice Virtuality and Collaborative Management

Vertical integration is an increasingly archaic and uncompetitive concept. Companies can no longer afford to do

---

### OPERATIONAL INNOVATION: VIRTUALITY/OUTSOURCING

**AeroTech Service Group** of St. Louis, Missouri, has built a highly effective virtual factory with **McDonnell Douglas Aerospace**. AeroTech's open, flexible network enables users to perform collaborative tasks, such as the design and manufacture of complex prototype parts. The system, which was initially used by 50 McDonnell Douglas employees, is now shared by thousands of suppliers and partners. One of the examples of the network's success involves **UCAR Composites**, a tooling manufacturer. By directly tapping into the code necessary to produce parts for McDonnell Douglas via AeroTech's secure system, the cost of information transfer alone has fallen from $400.00 to $4.00; and transport time has fallen from days to seconds.*

*David M. Upton and Andrew McAfee, "The Real Virtual Factory," *Harvard Business Review,* July/August 1996.

---

everything internally and expect to be world-class at all of them. However, winning companies *have* to be world-class in everything. That's where outsourcing comes in. By leveraging *focused* core competencies (superior infrastructures, cost structures, experience, and specific management skills), networks of service providers create a stronger suite of capabilities than their customers could develop on their own. Thus, in addition to making it possible to leverage world-class resources, the resulting virtuality helps companies increase flexibility and manage capacity, capability, and cost. Collaborating (and aligning processes) with suppliers, channel partners (and even competitors in some instances) is one sure way to drive costs out of the channel and system.

Shifting trends in channel management also strengthen the case for virtuality. This is because marketplace power is quickly becoming a function of channel dominance, and many companies are seeking to operate—and dominate—in multiple channels. However, channel dominance means matching operations to the local environment (demand, buying patterns, customs, and infrastructures), which vary. These characteristics explain why partnerships (a.k.a., virtuality) are increasingly key to channel dominance. For example, a computer company may increase its leadership and reduce its cost in the mass-merchandising channel by teaming with a partner that sells consumer electronics and faxes. They might also team with a company that can configure and deliver computers (e.g., a value-added reseller) in a particular channel. "Teaming" could mean anything from joint procurement to joint delivery and consolidation to joint trade promotion and returns management.

Another strong argument for virtuality comes from the fact that bigger continues to mean better. The larger you are, the better are your chances of market or channel domination. It's the law of increasing returns: economies of scale often contribute to supply chain excellence. And counterintuitive as it might seem, virtuality is, at its core, an attempt to gain scale—not unlike strategic alliances, mergers, or joint ventures. Put another way, virtuality helps companies to grow without investing in expensive infrastructure and fixed costs. For example, a smaller company might work with Procter & Gamble to supply Wal-Mart, or it might team with UPS to supply retailers or households. By leveraging UPS's infrastructure, they would gain the distribution advantages of a company that is many times their size. Many companies that leverage such a teaming approach also get price breaks from common suppliers. It's a mathematical balance between costs and service. In the future, there will be more (or, at least, as many) opportunities to innovate *between* companies as *within* companies.

---

*"Counterintuitive as it might seem, virtuality is, at its core, an attempt to gain scale—not unlike strategic alliances, mergers, or joint ventures."*

---

The key to virtuality and collaborative management is excellent management skills and the will to experiment (calculated risk taking). Outsourcing and partnerships do not

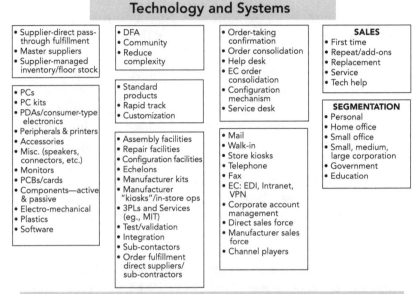

## Technology and Systems

| | | | |
|---|---|---|---|
| • Supplier-direct pass-through fulfillment<br>• Master suppliers<br>• Supplier-managed inventory/floor stock | • DFA<br>• Community<br>• Reduce complexity | • Order-taking confirmation<br>• Order consolidation<br>• Help desk<br>• EC order consolidation<br>• Configuration mechanism<br>• Service desk | **SALES**<br>• First time<br>• Repeat/add-ons<br>• Replacement<br>• Service<br>• Tech help |
| • PCs<br>• PC kits<br>• PDAs/consumer-type electronics<br>• Peripherals & printers<br>• Accessories<br>• Misc. (speakers, connectors, etc.)<br>• Monitors<br>• PCBs/cards<br>• Components—active & passive<br>• Electro-mechanical<br>• Plastics<br>• Software | • Standard products<br>• Rapid track<br>• Customization | | **SEGMENTATION**<br>• Personal<br>• Home office<br>• Small office<br>• Small, medium, large corporation<br>• Government<br>• Education |
| | • Assembly facilities<br>• Repair facilities<br>• Configuration facilities<br>• Echelons<br>• Manufacturer kits<br>• Manufacturer "kiosks"/in-store ops<br>• 3PLs and Services (eg., MIT)<br>• Test/validation<br>• Integration<br>• Sub-contactors<br>• Order fulfillment direct suppliers/sub-contractors | • Mail<br>• Walk-in<br>• Store kiosks<br>• Telephone<br>• Fax<br>• EC: EDI, Intranet, VPN<br>• Corporate account management<br>• Direct sales force<br>• Manufacturer sales force<br>• Channel players | |

### Joint fulfillment and asset sharing with other companies: complementary products, service, etc.

**Figure 2.13** Moving to virtual operations requires several key decisions: Focus? Segmentation? Management? Logistically separate operations? Where do we partner? Where do we outsource? Should vendors supply? They require increased and better management, not less management.

mean less management; they actually demand more and better management to ensure transparency to the customer. A company must make a whole host of hard decisions along its supply chain to move toward a virtual structure. Figure 2.13 illustrates these decisions and options in a computer company. Some are analytical, but all are strategic and cost/margin-driven.

## ➤ 9. Exploit Electronic Commerce

Electronic commerce is the result of some of the most exciting business/technology innovations to come along in years. And it is changing the supply chain. Briefly, electronic commerce is the buying, selling, and tracking of goods and services on the Internet or, for that matter, any Web-based technology. It represents a huge opportunity for many and a threat to some. For example, traditional supply chain structures rely on set channels at the downstream level for dis-tribution and "one-to-a-few" relationships upstream for procurement (one buyer using a few suppliers for a particular commodity, or relatively few for all procurement activities). For the most part, distribution channels have been controlled by a few companies (e.g., retailers, wholesalers, distributors, resellers), except when they have been challenged and displaced by "direct fulfillment manufacturers." Electronic commerce provides the means to bypass these points and to introduce a whole new channel: many-to-many. An example would be many companies sourcing material from a large number of suppliers that post their offerings and prices on the Web or in a catalog. Customers can view and compare goods electronically and buy as needed. What's more, companies that were too small to penetrate existing (physical) channels can now use this new electronic channel to market, display, and sell their goods. Electronic commerce will have a tremendous impact on the supply chain, with a large number of applications.

For instance, in procurement, which is traditionally handled through a company's regular supplier network, *electronic auctioning* changes the supplier-management equation. Companies can source commodities on the Internet and buy immediately, based on price and availability (thus saving significant money). They can also deal with more suppliers, and leverage new service benchmarks to recast some as purveyors of commodities. The net change is two new supplier categories: the *few partners* and the *many commodity vendors,* a change from the current practice of supplier consolidation and partnering across the board.

Overall, it will be a short time before existing problems such as security are solved and credit card and account trans-

actions take place in a large-scale manner. Figure 2.14 illustrates some applications of electronic commerce along the
supply chain. One consequence is the emergence of a "supply Web" or "demand/supply Web." This implies the ability
of key customers to have communities of suppliers and to
collaboratively plan, forecast, and replenish on as much of a
real-time basis as possible.

Electronic commerce does threaten numerous categories
of players, particularly middlemen (wholesalers, distributors, and resellers) that add little value to the product or service. The trend toward disintermediation also endangers
companies whose products are commodities, or near commodities, and those price-oriented businesses that compete
on a global basis. "Commodities" here refers to products that
can be represented and compared to other products digitally,
and shipped easily. (Contrary to the preachings of value-
added resellers and distributors, this *is* a large category.) In

| Marketing and Sales | Customer Service |
|---|---|
| ➤ On-line product information | ➤ Repairs, returns, replace- |
| ➤ Electronic selling | ment |
| ➤ Security and encryption | ➤ On-site fix |
| ➤ Product suite offerings/ | ➤ Technical/user support |
| electronic supermarkets | ➤ Product, usage information |
| | ➤ Tracking/status information |

| Procurement/ Transportation/Logistics | Replenishment and Inventory Management |
|---|---|
| ➤ Electronic auctioning, | ➤ Least-cost, high-availability |
| bidding | replenishment |
| ➤ Least-cost transportation | ➤ Product usage, demand |
| ➤ Least-cost point-to-point | information |
| delivery | ➤ Status/visibility and spot |
| ➤ Least-cost point warehousing | demand requirements |

**Figure 2.14** Some examples of electronic commerce applications
in the supply chain.

response, these players must create differentiation by adding value along three dimensions: the product, the information, or the function/process (Figure 2.15). Adding this value—creating the product/service "bundle" and taking over the customer's processes (functional value-add)—is probably the only way for traditional suppliers and middlemen who deal in commodity products to survive.

For companies that fail to create value-based differentiation, disintermediation is inevitable. Recognizing this, some distributors and resellers are becoming "master channel managers," providing and managing electronic commerce channels for others. Electronic commerce is the next supply chain battleground, and it will change the nature of competition.

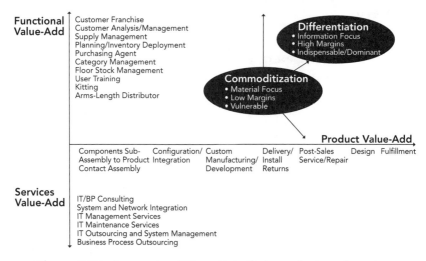

**Figure 2.15** Companies differentiate their products and services from commodities by adding new value.

## ➤ 10. Leverage People

Today's U.S. transportation or procurement manager will not necessarily morph into a great international supply chain manager. In this highly complex and codependent world of information, processes, channels, and customers, the skills of a supply chain executive are vital, specialized, and broad. The very best will be:

➤ Multicultural. They will possess a multinational perspective.

➤ Multifunctional. They will comprehend all aspects of the supply chain, as well as the supply chain's business, market, and competitive impacts.

➤ Knowledgeable in practices and results across industries.

➤ Able to motivate and manage a wide variety of people: employees as well as external suppliers, partners, and providers.

➤ Able to conceptualize solutions and implement them.

➤ Focused on margins, revenue enhancement, working and fixed capital, and the total cost and business implications of all decisions across the enterprise. They will understand the business and operational models.

➤ Highly familiar with the functional implications of information systems and technology.

➤ Able to recruit, build teams, and motivate cross-geography and cross-discipline teams.

These attributes (which combine functional, IT, and people-management skills) represent a radical shift in perspective. Human resource perceptions must migrate from manager to leader—from international executive to global executive—and from logistics director to supply chain business and information officer. This metamorphosis requires careful development, rotation, recruiting of key people, and a workforce that is motivated and rewarded according to business results and equity. The right people can accomplish nearly anything with the right focus and the right support.

## ➤ 11. Operationalize New Product Introductions and Phaseouts

An often overlooked facet of supply chain management is its integration with new product development. The hazards of ignoring this connection are multifold:

➤ Lack of availability and lost sales in the crucial product introduction/ramp-up stage (and, as a consequence, potential new-product failure)

➤ Excess and obsolete inventory in the product phaseout stage

➤ Entry opportunities for competitors when the company is early in the product/technology life cycle

➤ Increased cost and longer product stabilization time

➤ Higher supply chain costs (for example, in one case where multiple sources of supply were not planned for in a multigeography rollout)

➤ Uncompetitive cost structures during the life of the product if manufacturing, sourcing, and deployment factors were not considered during life cycle planning

➤ Excess spare inventory and customer dissatisfaction if end-of-service-life issues are not considered

Figure 2.16 illustrates some of the key supply chain life cycle decisions that must be made *at the outset* of the development and phase review process.

## ➤ 12. Mass Customize and Postpone

The basis of mass customization is moving final stages of production or finishing (the point where product becomes

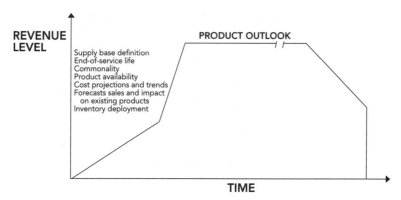

**Figure 2.16** Several key decisions help integrate the new-product development and introduction process and supply chain management.

unique or can be dedicated to a specific customer) closer to the customer and, thereby, minimizing SKUs and product proliferation. The mass customizer builds and configures to order and pushes the point of order and product differentiation as far downstream as possible, as near to the cus-

---

### OPERATIONAL INNOVATION: MASS CUSTOMIZATION

**ESEC Group,** maker of automatic assembly equipment for the semiconductor industry, has implemented a worldwide "sales configurator" system. The system allows a salesperson to produce a complete order in a standard format from anywhere in the world. The software checks for accuracy by assessing manufacturability. Some of the benefits that ESEC Group has realized are increased order accuracy, improved work flow and efficiency, stronger customer loyalty, and the ability of salespeople to focus on incoming business rather than managing existing orders.*

*Marty Weil, "Marching Orders," *Manufacturing Systems,* 15, no. 5 (May 1997): 34–41.

---

### OPERATIONAL INNOVATION: MASS CUSTOMIZATION

Several years ago, **National Bicycle,** a subsidiary of Matsushita Electric, began offering customers customized bicycles at close-to-mass-production prices. Customers visit a dealership and choose a bike from a selection of two million options for style, size, color, and components. In two weeks, they receive the customized bicycle. Soon after, National Bicycle increased its share of the Japanese sports bicycle market from 5 to 29 percent.*

*Harvard Business Review, 19 March 1997.

---

tomer as possible (as practiced by Hewlett-Packard with printers and Braun with shavers, a process known as "delayed product differentiation"). If the customers can actually do it themselves, so much the better. Remember, mass customization and postponement can apply to many aspects of a product, product configuration (computers, for instance), color, style, shape, cut, packaging, key features and add-ons, or even delivery. In net, mass customization is driven by what is important to the customer: *what differentiates the sale.*

Mass customization is not a trivial undertaking, and it is obviously not for every product (particularly nondifferentiated commodities). It involves redesigning products for maximum commonality, shipment in the "prefinal" state, and production processes designed for maximum downstream flexibility. The customization can be done at the retail outlet level (like Levi Strauss), at the regional geography level (like Benetton), or at the plant level (like Dell). It simply depends on the nature of the product, the process, and the channel. Mass customization will be crucial in the near future as a vehicle to reduce overall costs, increase customer service levels and satisfaction, and be a prime market differentiator.

## ■ SUMMARY

More and more, leading companies are defined by their ability to identify key business mandates and, based on those observations, develop innovative supply chain responses. Those responses demonstrate a profound shift from the traditional supply-driven focus to an operationally excellent state that is customer-centric and supply-aware (see Figure 2.17).

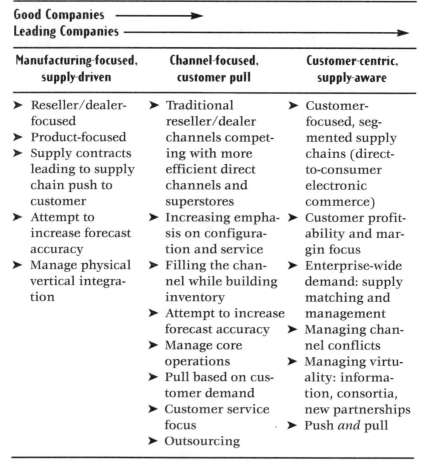

| Good Companies ──────➤ | | |
| Leading Companies ──────────────────────────➤ | | |
| **Manufacturing-focused, supply-driven** | **Channel-focused, customer pull** | **Customer-centric, supply-aware** |
| ➤ Reseller/dealer-focused<br>➤ Product-focused<br>➤ Supply contracts leading to supply chain push to customer<br>➤ Attempt to increase forecast accuracy<br>➤ Manage physical vertical integration | ➤ Traditional reseller/dealer channels competing with more efficient direct channels and superstores<br>➤ Increasing emphasis on configuration and service<br>➤ Filling the channel while building inventory<br>➤ Attempt to increase forecast accuracy<br>➤ Manage core operations<br>➤ Pull based on customer demand<br>➤ Customer service focus<br>➤ Outsourcing | ➤ Customer-focused, segmented supply chains (direct-to-consumer electronic commerce)<br>➤ Customer profitability and margin focus<br>➤ Enterprise-wide demand: supply matching and management<br>➤ Managing channel conflicts<br>➤ Managing virtuality: information, consortia, new partnerships<br>➤ Push *and* pull |

**Figure 2.17** Excellence is crafting a set of customer-centric, supply-aware responses to key business issues.

---

**ASK YOUR MANAGERS**

1. How do each of the 12 issues affect your operations today? How will they affect them tomorrow?

2. Have you planned for these?

3. What (*precisely*) are your responses to them?

4. What are you doing about the key imperatives and who is accountable?

5. What are the metrics for each imperative and who is accountable?

6. What is your performance against these key metrics?

7. What are your plans? What resources are needed?

8. Have you focused on a few key imperatives?

---

Although many good companies will focus on customer-pull responses, *leading* companies will apply both push and pull to maximize revenues and minimize costs. (Yes, flooding the channel at reduced margins in some instances is acceptable for companies that practice demand/supply matching.) This is a strategy that genuinely merges operational (e.g., supply chain) excellence with the company's overall goal: continuously higher shareholder value.

## ■ ENDNOTE

[1]Geoffrey A. Moore, *Inside the Tornado*. New York: HarperBusiness, 1995.

# Chapter 3

# Planning for Value: Synchronizing Demand and Supply

Demand/supply planning and management is the nervous system of company operations. It is the key to achieving targeted customer service levels, inventory levels, and margins; it is also the key to managing system-wide capacity. If there is a single, end-to-end process that must be enterprise wide in scope, integration, and accountability, this is it.

Optimizing supply and demand requires *managing* as well as planning. The process must be designed, owned, monitored, and measured. Growth, profitability, and customer service must be balanced carefully. Most important, operations must be customer-centric and supply-aware, rather than supply-, production-, or forecast-driven.

Effective demand/supply planning has eight primary tenets:

1. *Ensure high-level accountability.* In all companies, a senior executive must be accountable for results. Demand/supply management is a process that comes together at the top, so it must be credentialized by

executive management. This involves a great deal more than assigning ownership; it involves a behavioral change, with metrics that are tied to the operating plan.

2. *Combine demand and supply planning.* Supply chains that are focused on the operating plan are simultaneously demand driven and supply managed. Contrary to prevailing rhetoric, an "all-pull" system is unnecessary, unmanageable, and unrealistic. This is why demand and supply planning should be combined within a single function that 1) includes the input of key customers and suppliers, and 2) reports to a senior executive. Moreover, demand/supply plans should have both a long-term outlook and a daily tactical update. And they should consider all inputs, including price and demand changes, and new product "commits" and "decommits."

3. *Eliminate the impact of the product forecast.* Rather than trying to improve their demand forecasts, companies should work to de-emphasize them. This is because highly effective supply chains with fast cycle times reduce the need for demand forecasts, which are never accurate anyway. The focus of the demand/supply process must be on answering real-time demand and cutting cycle times. In turn, the forecasting emphasis should be on managing capacity and procuring materials, rather than on predicting demand.

4. *Create a common language and a focus on commonality.* Commonality is the keystone of supply chains that are flexible and cost effective. A supply chain–wide focus on uniformity—for example, a common product language—will bring about larger and more dramatic savings than almost any other initiative. It will also make end-to-end demand and supply planning much easier.

5. *Treat customers unequally.* Based on cost to serve, cost to sell, profitability, and complexity of demands, some customers are a great deal less equal than others. Thus,

they should be segmented and serviced in a way that does not make a relationship with them strategically or economically disadvantageous.

6. *Manage backward as well as forward: plan for spares and returns.* Companies need to manage the logistics of returns—such as spares, repairs, customer service, and warranty management—with the same intensity and commitment as forward supply chain management.

7. *Replace inventory with information and analysis: deploy smaller, easily implementable, functional systems that share common, accurate data.* Information and analysis are essential to managing the product pipeline. They are best optimized with smaller, rapidly implemented, integrated applications with an accompanying focus on enterprise-wide data accuracy, integrity, and commonality.

8. *Focus on transparency in planning and deployment.* Transparency to the consumer should be paramount, no matter how virtual the supply chain. The customer does not care *how* the product gets to him. He does, however, care if the product arrives late, damaged, or not at all.

## ■ LINKING DEMAND AND SUPPLY

In practice, integrated demand/supply management is a fairly complex but necessary process that comprises three major components: supply planning, demand planning, and inventory deployment (Figure 3.1).

Supply planning covers procurement, capacity, and capability. It is driven by margin targets, which, in turn, are influenced by commodity prices, capacity costs, costs of supply, flexibility, and availability (uninterrupted supply). Supply planning also implies the planning of all materials and the evaluation of product technologies, industry capabilities/

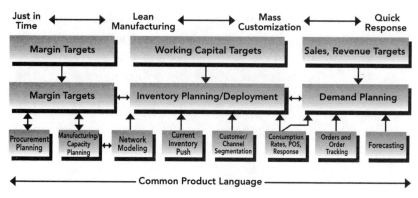

**Figure 3.1** Demand/supply planning.

capacities, and total acquisition costs. The supply-planning ideal is JIT supply, in which inventory is never on the company's books until it is consumed (or, better yet, sold and paid for by the customer).

Demand planning, on the other hand, is driven by sales and revenue targets and, in some instances, mixed profitability targets. To many companies, however, demand planning is a forecasting process. This is a faulty and often dangerous perspective. In reality, forecasting should be a small part of a much larger process that emphasizes quick response, order management, and inventory optimization strategies for satisfying customer demand in a cost-effective manner.

> *"To reduce dependency on the forecast, emphasize demand/supply management and reduce operational cycle time."*

Inventory deployment is part of the demand-planning cycle and incorporates decisions about where and when to deploy inventory, how much inventory to deploy, and for how long. Inventory deployment is based on customer demand, the supply position, and marketing programs and promotions. It must be managed by customer segment and channel at a strategic and highly tactical level. Ideally, an inventory deployment process will orchestrate cost-effective and responsive material flows throughout the enterprise. Its emphasis will be on *velocity*—just-in-time from the suppliers and quick response to the customers—and on driving internal, lean manufacturing and mass customization efforts.

The bottom line is that demand/supply management is not about fulfilling customer needs. It is about *making money. It is about achieving the operating plan* and the metrics by which the process (and its "owners") are measured, managed, and linked to the operating metrics of the company. For these lofty (but necessary) goals to be attained, demand/supply planning must simultaneously:

➤ Maintain (and plan for) customer service and support for all segments and channels.

➤ Achieve lowest total costs and targeted margins, while assuring uninterrupted supply.

➤ Attain targeted working capital levels and reductions for products in all stages of their market cycles, including end-of-life, service, and spares. It must also target inventory velocity explicitly.

➤ Manage to optimum capacity levels (internal and external) and market coverage, including outsourcing and copacking alternatives.

➤ Set realistic targets for working capital, fixed capital, costs, and commodity prices.

Conversely, the costs of poor demand/supply planning can be huge. Their consequences include:

➤ High and uncompetitive working capital levels, which can result in inventory levels that are too high, too low, too expensive, too old, obsolete, or misaligned with demand. Cash that could be used to fund investments, efficiencies, new products, or market expansion gets tied up in nonproductive ways.

➤ Interrupted material supplies, stockouts, and poor availability.

➤ Lack of flexibility and responsiveness to market needs.

➤ Excess supply chain complexity.

➤ Uncompetitive total delivered costs after taxes.

➤ Inability to meet committed service levels consistently and efficiently, which leads to lost customers and lost sales.

In net, poor demand/supply planning produces ineffective, inefficient, or broken supply chains. To keep poor demand/supply planning from happening, consider the following profiles of demand/supply planning's eight key tenets.

## ➤ 1. Ensure High-Level Accountability for Demand/Supply Management

At most companies, an operations strategy *evolves*. Ongoing financial concerns—reducing labor costs, for example—usually drive the evolution. With such a nonstrategic strategy, it shouldn't be surprising that most businesses also delegate planning and deployment to manager-level staff or systems operators. However, by doing so, they minimize the significance of demand and supply integration and set the stage for the enterprise-wide consequences of poor demand/supply planning.

To be competitive, companies must address demand/supply management at the top. They must combine demand planning and supply planning at a high level and credentialize it through the involvement and accountability of executive management. The executive level is where all of the supply chain's far-reaching activities can be examined and synthesized. Also, it is where trade-offs and conflicts (e.g., balancing

---

### OPERATIONAL INNOVATION: INTEGRATING SUPPLY AND DEMAND

**Ames,** a large manufacturer of garden tools, and **Ace Hardware Corp.,** a giant retailer, created a new approach to integrating their supply- and demand-planning processes. The new approach manages and warehouses inventory between the manufacturer and the retailer. Ames produces snow shovels exclusively for Ace and delivers them exactly when and where the retailer needs them. Ames is able to monitor and keep track of Ace's warehouse using its Manugistics software. Major benefits include higher fill rates and lower inventory.*

*Tom Stein, "Orders from Chaos," *Information Week,* no. 636 (23 June 1997): 44–6, 50 ff.

---

growth, profitability, and customer service) should be identified and resolved—not at the customer, operational, or supplier levels. In fact, it is only at the senior staff level that these decisions and trade-offs can be made and subsequently linked to a strategy for achieving the operating plan. Surprisingly, it doesn't matter where within the executive suite demand/supply functions report. We have seen that rotating responsibility among senior staff works very well in some companies.

In a sense, the demand/supply plan is a blueprint set by executive management for achieving the operating plan. An executive-driven, demand/supply–planning process will chart the most effective flow of goods and materials through the *complete* supply chain, including trading partner and alliance chains.

### ➤ 2. Combine Demand and Supply Planning

There are many reasons to integrate demand and supply planning; however, the major one is to *resolve conflicting objectives.*

Consider that the drivers of supply planning are fundamentally different from those of demand planning. Supply planning is driven chiefly by margin targets, which, in turn, are derived from raw material costs, pricing strategies, and the need for an uninterrupted stream of goods or materials. Demand planning, on the other hand, is driven chiefly by sales targets and the company's ability to reach them. These targets are based (hopefully) on estimates of market demand. Integrated (or at least highly coordinated) demand/supply planning reconciles the missions of these separate areas.

> *"The main reason to integrate demand and supply planning is to resolve conflicting objectives."*

In several instances, different companies in the end-to-end chain control different areas. For example, in the computer industry's reseller channel, key commodity suppliers direct the "source/buy" chain, whereas resellers (and some distributors) control the "replenish" cycle. Thus, it is wishful thinking to believe that one company oversees the entire chain in all circumstances. This is why integrated demand/supply planning is needed to coordinate tightly three supply chains and their divergent objectives (Figure 3.2):

➤ Source and buy (efficiently and "just-in-time")

➤ Make and deliver (per the customer order or to planned availability)

➤ Replenish (quick response to customer demand)

For long-term capacity strategies and supply planning, the horizon for integrated, high-level demand/supply planning should extend for one to two years at an aggregate level. Revisions are advisable at six-month increments at the granular (product family) level, with weekly or daily updates made at a detailed product level. Weekly meetings of all players help to focus the organization on the plan and to make corrections

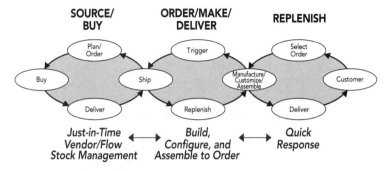

**Figure 3.2** Tight linkages are the key to effective supply chain management.

resulting from changing market demand and supply constraints.

Tying this process to the order stream is the key to real-time demand management. Real-time order and configuration management make this even more potent as a competitive weapon. This is where decisions are made according to actual customer demand patterns and not based on some inaccurate forecast or demand wish list. Figure 3.3 illustrates the process, which must consider all inputs, be inclusive, and comprehend

## Process Flow

| The Operating Plan Metrics and Focused Metrics: Performance Management |
|---|

| Operating Plan Targets | Order Book | ┌ ─ ─ ─ ─ ─ ┐ | Geographic Transfers | Master Plan |
|---|---|---|---|---|
| Systemwide Inventory Status | Generate/Update Sales Forecast | Demand Plan | Subcontractor Selection Allocation | Procurement Requirements |
| Customer Service Requirements | | | | Production Requirements |
| Procurement Plans and Supply Position | New Product Phase-In/Out | | Inventory Deployment | Inventory Deployment |
| Supplier Position and Flexibility | Spares Plan | Demand/ Supply Plan Deployment | Marketing/ Channel Programs | Subcontractor Schedules |
| Production Schedules and Position (Internal/External) | Supply Plan | └ ─ ─ ─ ─ ─ ┘ | | |
| Distribution Requirements | Channel Stock | | | |
| New Products | | 2+1 year + 6 month Outlook + Monthly Review + Daily Update | | |
| Commits/Decommits | | Product Sales/Customer Service/Channel Segmentation Multiple Iterations/"What-if"s | | |

**Figure 3.3** Demand/supply planning considers all inputs, using multiple iterations to produce the master plan, which maximizes availability, margins, and working capital, while balancing growth and profitability.

---

## OPERATIONAL INNOVATION: INTEGRATING SUPPLY AND DEMAND

**Reebok International Ltd.** is moving to on-line connections (bar code and EDI) and collaboration with suppliers, distributors, and retailers to integrate its supply and demand planning. Results include reduced cycle times, inventories, and costs, as well as improved customer responsiveness. One particularly notable benefit is the company's improved ability to react quickly to changes in market demand. Other apparel companies practicing integrated demand/supply planning are:

➤ **Guess? Inc.,** which is using EDI with Dillard's, Federated, and other department store retailers. At its 125 retail outlets, Guess? uses bar-code scanners linked to local Windows NT servers to send electronic data to its suppliers for replenishment.

➤ **VF Services, Inc.,** the world's largest publicly held apparel company, which has strong EDI links with Wal-Mart Stores, Inc. Every evening, VF receives POS data from Wal-Mart via satellite for manufacturing planning and other purposes.*

*Nick Wrenden, "Supply Chain Get Better Links," *Communications Week,* (16 June 1997): 86–7.

---

segmentation and service strategies to generate the master plan (the plan that everybody in the company signs up for and executes).

### *Push versus Pull*

As discussed later (and in Chapter 2), a key tenet of profitable growth and cost reduction is that *all customers are not equal.* Certainly, EMV-focused companies work to meet the precise demands of customers; they also practice good cost management by stratifying service levels based on customer criteria such as profitability, cost of service, volume of business, and strategic value. In other words, they provide different levels of customer service (delivery, lead times, pricing) by customer segment or channel segment. In many instances, because their forecasts—like everyone else's—are inaccurate, they always have some need to push existing inventories through the pipeline via marketing promotions, cross-selling, new "bundled" product combinations, pricing incentives, or lead-time delivery incentives.

Despite these realities, "push" is becoming passé in the lexicon of many academics and supply chain strategists. This is a problem. Demand-driven approaches are necessary up to a point; however, wholesale commitment to a pull-oriented supply chain is misplaced. "All-pull," after all, implies that supplies are highly flexible and virtually unlimited, that there are no costs (or premiums) tied to discontinuity, and that demand must be satisfied absolutely. Like a genie from a bottle, any level of demand can result in the instant summoning of needed supply. It is obvious that although an all-pull system may be the ideal, often it is economically unwise in terms of working capital investment, capacity usage, total costs, and margins.

Effective demand/supply planning, on the other hand, is simultaneously *demand driven and supply aware* (or supply constrained). It is the result of synthesizing procurement planning, manufacturing capacity planning, demand planning, inventory planning, and deployment.

## ➤ 3. Eliminate the Impact of the Product Forecast

An integrated demand/supply process will help deal with one of supply chain management's most historically fruitless endeavors: creating an accurate, useful, product-level forecast. Forecasts are always inaccurate; even if they weren't, they are only one small piece of demand/supply planning. Companies seeking to forecast the use of a product with highly stable demand may come close. But in the real world, few products experience highly stable demand profiles; far more often, the demand mix is erratic. In these cases, responding by trying to forecast the mix—or attempting to forecast each and every product configuration—only makes the situation worse. Overall, the greater the instability of forecasted items, the greater the need to tie *actual* demand from customers into your scheduling, delivering, and deployment operations through real-time order management.

When demand for an item is inherently unstable, it is more productive to forecast the key *components* that make up the product. Forecasting component consumption allows companies to link usage or order data to the manufacturing floor. This has the potential to accelerate turnaround (quick response), improve product customization, provide realistic plans to suppliers, and neutralize the impact of an inherently inaccurate forecast.

In broad terms, "the lower the level of the forecast (in terms of product detail), the more inherently inaccurate it is." Therefore, it can be a waste of time, resources, and competitive effort to seek improved forecast accuracy for products. This is another reason why building a 100-percent demand-driven supply chain is imprudent. (In today's jargon-riddled world, though, people are starting to refer to the supply chain as the "demand chain," as if euphemisms lead to operational excellence.) Highly successful, demand-driven operations require highly accurate forecasts, highly efficient asset deployment, or very short cycle times. However, highly accurate forecasts virtually don't exist! Therefore, the focus should be on eliminating (or at least reducing) dependency on the forecast by tightly coupling order and manufacturing/fulfillment processes and reducing cycle times within operations. In other words, manage realistically and efficiently by *linking demand with supply*. The less predictable the demand, the greater the importance of linking customer demand (in the form of customer orders via real-time order management) directly into the manufacturing floor.

This response, however, is dependent on the company achieving quick cycle times in its manufacturing and supply operations. The quicker the cycle time, the easier it is to respond to changing demand patterns on a product level. Naturally, this is easier said than done. Of course, a company can always *buy* reduced lead or response times by stocking excess inventory, but this defeats the overall purpose. Real cycle time reduction is a function of tough and creative initiatives in manufacturing, component, and industrial engineering.

Finally, *forecasts do help in certain areas,* such as supply planning, capacity planning, and establishing working capital targets. Here, accountability for *one* forecast should rest with *one* person or *one* group of people representing marketing, finance, operations, and sales. These forecasts should be driven partly by statistically based ideas about demand and partly by working capital targets, new product plans and phaseouts, existing and projected inventory, and sales targets. These, in turn, become the financial drivers of a company's procurement, distribution, and manufacturing plans.

### Aligning Processes across Companies

Integrated demand/supply planning can be greatly helped by *aligning processes and systems with suppliers and key customers* (Figure 3.4). This is a prerequisite for such practices and programs as category management and vendor-managed

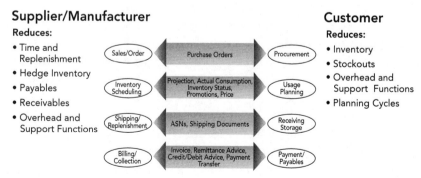

**Figure 3.4** Aligning processes and systems with suppliers and customers.

inventory (VMI). Furthermore, it reduces dependency on inaccurate forecasts. A manufacturer's inventory-scheduling decisions, for example, relate to its customers' procurement/ supply-planning processes. Shipping and replenishment must connect with customers' receiving and storage. Billing and collection must be synchronized with customer payment and payables.

This linkage benefits suppliers through reduced replenishment times, fewer receivables, and less redundancy. Customers enjoy leaner inventories and fewer stockouts. Both get more efficient overhead and support functions. The ultimate setting for this linkage is one process composed of customers, manufacturers, and suppliers, and based on a seamless exchange of information. This level of cooperation is seldom seen today, but it is the direction in which some leading companies are moving. The principal stumbling block, of course, is that customers do not want to give their suppliers control of critical functions and information. Often, there is a good reason for this reluctance; however, with adequate safeguards, management processes, and metrics, suppliers can assume greater control of their customers' processes and materials. When this happens, operations become more virtual, and demand/supply planning gets easier.

### Let the Vendor Do It

Vendor-managed inventory is a good way to connect demand and supply planning. By making a supplier responsible for monitoring, consumption, planning, and supply, manufacturers can jettison much of their need for replenishment planning and executing, as well as forecasting.

Vendor-managed inventory is usually a collaborative effort between suppliers and their top-tier customers. Programs can range from replenishing a customer's distribution center to direct store deliveries and shelf-space replenishment. With VMI, vendors manage the physical flow of product to the immediate customer, and both parties manage real-time information flow throughout the channel. Such programs work best in industries in which there is a steady and high volume of product flow, such as retail and consumer products. They have also been used extensively in manufacturing, in which suppliers manage floor stock for use in production. However, forms of VMI are also gaining popularity in the electronics and high-technology sectors, in which the value of inventory per unit is high and many products have demand unpredictability throughout their (usually short) life cycles.

It is important to note that VMI fundamentally changes how vendors and customers do business (Figure 3.5). In most VMI relationships, new approaches to order management, manufacturing, picking, packing, shipping, invoicing, and even displaying are essential. However, three maxims define VMI under *all* circumstances:

➤ Sell-through POS or consumption data—as near to real time as possible—must be made available to vendors.

| Efficient Vendor-Managed Inventory Programs Benefit . . . | |
| --- | --- |
| Vendors Through . . . | Customers Through . . . |
| Smoother customer demand (more efficient usage of resources, reduced surge capacity required, reduced raw and finished goods inventories) | Reduced inventory levels<br>Reduced operating costs<br>Increased sales because of higher in-stock rates |
| Improved communication with customers<br>Increased sales via higher in-stock rates<br>Customer sales data available for market analysis | Improved communication and cooperation with vendors |
| Opportunity to influence merchandising and category management and provide value-added services | Vendor assistance with merchandising and category management |

**Figure 3.5** Vendor-managed inventory programs can benefit suppliers and customers.

➤ Vendors must have a lean supply chain capability that allows them to replenish quickly and in small lots at better-than-competitive prices.

➤ Vendors must have the information systems ability to monitor customer-site and system-wide inventories and sales, and be able to ship/replenish product without purchase orders.

Companies that do a poor job of demand/supply management in their own operations will probably hurt themselves by attempting to manage their customers' inventories. In effect, they will be expanding poor processes and management into a less forgiving arena. The benefits from succeeding, however, can be significant to both vendors and customers, focusing the power of two (or more) organizations on merchandising, selling, and replenishing products at highest availability and least cost.

Category management (CM) is an extended version of VMI: vendor-centered management of complete product categories on behalf of a customer. Like VMI, CM requires superior administration, excellent vendor-customer communication, and sophisticated information control. The key benefit for suppliers—in addition to stronger profit potential—is a chance to reduce their reliance on retailers as the primary interpreter of consumer needs and preferences. Category management also dramatically increases the customer's (retailer's) costs of switching to other vendors by strengthening dependency on the supplier.

## ➤ 4. Create a Common Language and a Focus on Commonality

Complexity (in products and processes) and a lack of commonality in products create a ton of enterprise-wide

> ## OPERATIONAL INNOVATION: CUSTOMER SEGMENTATION/STRATIFICATION
>
> **FedEx** has long led its industry in segmenting the customer base and designing specific-service products to meet different needs. For example, priority overnight, as well as one-, two-, and three-day services, are provided at different price points— all with value-added services wrapped around these offerings.

inefficiencies and headaches. Too many unique products, components, and part numbers result directly in higher levels of inventory, excess and obsolete costs, and planning complexity. To reduce complexity and increase efficiency, companies can adopt three major initiatives:

1. *Reduce the number of parts that go into each product and increase the commonality of those parts.* In supply chain management, "proliferation" is a bad word. So is "unique." The goal is to make individual products that have fewer components, and to design the maximum number of common components across those products.

2. *Rationalize products.* Few companies should aspire to have something for everyone. A better goal is to attract a large number of customers to a small number of *highly customizable* end-item products that were built using common components and common processes. This is the essence of mass customization: not 100 distinct, discrete options, but 100 (or 1000) potential configurations, each with as few parts as possible. To make this happen, companies must begin by rationalizing their product lines based on margins, market size, regional requirements, and customer segments. The next step is to reconfigure and design manufacturing to segregate stages and to postpone the point of product-order allocation to the very end of the process.

**3.** *Create a common product language.* To make planning and deployment more effective and efficient, parties within and outside the company need to use the same language. Lack of a common product language is one of the most subtle and stubborn barriers to improved supply chain performance. In many companies, for example, configuration and part-numbering schemes begin with engineering. Manufacturing then makes up its own system, followed by marketing and later by sales. Outside the company, customers often insist on another scheme that is compatible with their numbering systems. Suppliers may also have their own. Finally, mergers and acquisitions often exacerbate the problem by proliferating systems across sites.

In either context, the result is separate or irreconcilable schemes across the supply chain—inside and external to the company. This translates to a significant number of problems with major financial impact: more inventories, redundant overhead, poor obsolescence management, fulfillment errors, materials shortages, ineffective tracking procedures, poor warranty and returns management, slow demand response, and overly complex data management.

> *"Lack of a common product language is one of the most subtle and stubborn barriers to improved supply chain performance."*

Not too many companies undertake comprehensive initiatives to develop common product languages. This is partly due to the sheer mass of such an undertaking, as well as the extra time, skills, tools, and level of interfunctional cooperation needed. However, the need to do *something* is growing. This is because most companies face a proliferation of product configurations and features on the one hand, and shorter technology and product life cycles on the other. Dealing with more products and components negatively impacts procurement, time/cost to assemble, and service. Additionally, shorter life cycles and increasing channel options force many companies to implement more (or more complicated) supply chains. Redundant numbering and incompatible naming conventions make these problems worse.

How much worse? According to some estimates, companies pay an extra $1500 to $6000 per year for each redundant part number. An average company has tens of thousands of SKUs. Larger companies often have hundreds of thousands. This is not pocket change.

Creating a common product language implies two things: 1) developing a single-configuration change management process across the company, and 2) creating part-numbering schemes between the customer and the supplier that are common or strongly linked and are structured around a consistent, global parts master. The key is expanding outward to build a company-wide—and then a supply chain–wide—set of standards, while leveraging technology to ensure consistency.

➤ **5. Treat Customers Unequally**

Customers have varying levels of desirability. That desirability may be a function of their strategic value, the volume of

---

**OPERATIONAL INNOVATION: CUSTOMER SEGMENTATION/STRATIFICATION**

**Polaroid Corp.** changed its corporate structure from a product-focused organization to a market-oriented organization. Polaroid's organizational structure focuses on three "market-oriented" core areas: consumer, commercial, and new business. Activities are targeted at customer segmentation.*

*Newsbytes News Network (5 February 1996).

business they do, the profitability and total cost to serve them, the industry they represent, or their relevance to a supplier's core business. But the fact remains: clear levels of customer importance exist in the minds of all suppliers. However, many suppliers—especially the ones with mission statements of "delighting" customers with 100 percent on-time, demand-driven service—fail to operationalize that distinction. They don't see the large, bottom-line impact of service stratification or the benefits it could bestow on their planning and fulfillment processes.

To manage and match demand and supply effectively, companies must have margin-focused segmentation programs. These can be obtained in three ways: by customer, by channel, or by product line.

### Customer Segmentation

This means analyzing the total cost to sell and serve customer segments, followed by the development of discrete service programs that maximize margins. Some customers are money-losers for their suppliers. For one reason or another, they may be worth having as customers, but they are not profitable recipients of premium service or low prices. Services—like products—have price points: Companies need to focus their efforts on customers that make (or will make) them the most money.

### Channel Segmentation

Channel segmentation is similar. Many companies go to channels as a way to increase volume. Some are successful; others aren't. A few years ago, IBM and other computer makers tried (and failed) to implement a direct-delivery model.

Conversely, Dell once tried (and failed) to build a mass-merchandise channel. Companies must assess channels in the same way they do customers: by the potential each approach has to make money! Although it may be strategically important to be represented in a particular channel, a company can still provide varying levels of service and price, based on margin potential and cost to serve, unless they tackle the issues via logistically separate operations.

### *Product Line Segmentation*

Product line segmentation is probably the most complex strategy to implement, unless the lines are branded differently or sold through different channels. Essentially, it provides different levels of service and discounts by product line (in other words, different product/service bundles).

The most obvious means of differentiating service by customers and channels is to eliminate low-margin offerings completely. More common (and less painful) is developing stratified service and price levels that increase the potential for higher margins. For example, some customers get discounts, others get list price; some customers get more product, others don't; some customers get overnight delivery, others get five weeks; customers in one geographic area get a high level of service, customers in a different area don't. Some companies are experimenting with airline pricing, which is based on demand and availability. Finally, for customers that are desirable yet unprofitable, a company can choose to outsource the fulfillment process if it doesn't wish to make the investment. (See Figure 3.6.)

Any segmentation effort, however, requires high-level planning and deployment that is based on an accurate assessment of each customer's needs. Companies without this capability won't know where to focus critical (or limited) supply

| | Price Points, Service Levels | | | | Levers (Elements of the bundle) |
|---|---|---|---|---|---|
| | Geography | | | | ➤ Lead times |
| Product line/family | | | | | ➤ Price<br>➤ Availability<br>➤ Inventory levels |
| Channel | | | | | ➤ Delivery |
| Category | | | | | ➤ Services |

**Figure 3.6** Segmentation by geographic region cuts across product, channel, and customer categories.

elements. Consider that "A" customers are likely to command the bulk of available supplies, so their EMV-focused suppliers will plan for a quick response capability or sufficient inventory to meet Customer "A"'s quick-turnaround requirements. "B" customers, on the other hand, may have an altogether different service profile—with a different bundle of goods and services, different delivery modes (and/or channels), and more standard fulfillment schedules. On-hand inventory may not be necessary for "B" customers. Thus, longer lead times provide the opportunity to reduce carrying costs and service expenses by not having supplies readily available. Additionally, "B" customers may be more likely to order sporadically and in smaller lot sizes (that's probably what makes them "B" customers). By maximizing overall margins and sales potential, segmentation helps suppliers keep "B" customers as profitable sources of revenue.

## ➤ 6. Manage Backward as Well as Forward

In some industries, spares and returns can account for up to 35 percent of total inventory costs. With this level of cost, you'd think that spares and returns would be a significant focal point in most companies' planning and deployment strategies. They aren't. But there are several good reasons why they should be. For one thing, spares and returns tie up enormous amounts of working capital. Additionally, most companies seek to differentiate themselves through superior after-sales support. Insufficient attention to spares and returns can make that support even more costly and, from the customer's perspective, less effective. The point is: Spares and returns—including excess and obsolete goods and components—must be managed throughout the planning and deployment process (Figure 3.7).

A holistic spares-management process begins with product design, in which serviceability and modularity are built in and failure data are collected. The process continues into marketing, in which repair, warranty, and end-of-service-life (EOSL) policies are established. End-of-service life is a significant, yet regularly overlooked part of demand/supply planning. Some companies try to service everything they've ever made, ignoring the costs of related capabilities, tools, and

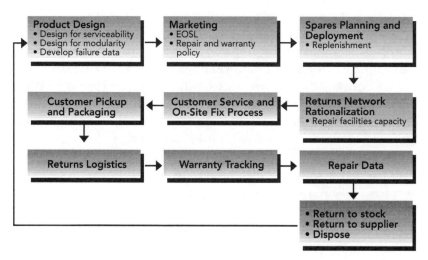

**Figure 3.7** The spares and returns process. These issues permeate the complete planning and deployment cycle.

inventory. In other words, it may be more cost-effective to give old customers a new product. In net, EOSL—like most supply chain management decisions—should be bottom-line driven and measurable. A financially grounded supply chain basis is needed for stocking spares, structuring replacement and warranty policies, extending or discontinuing service on certain products, and outsourcing aftermarket service. Basic decision parameters include:

➤ Production cost per unit/lot

➤ Projected excess and obsolete (E&O) estimate

➤ Product sales outlook

➤ Level of modularity/field-replaceable units (FRUs)

➤ Inventory-carrying cost

➤ New product introduction/line replacement

➤ Usage/mean time between failures (MTBFs) by segment/service location

Coordination with design and marketing will significantly improve spares planning and deployment. This entails identifying necessary projections and quantities of spares, and making them available when and where needed. These projections should cover replacements based on product or component failure rates, quick service response policies, and the projected volume of sales and promotions. All should be planned and managed by model, manufacturer, stocking location, service center, and (very importantly) customer segment. Managing by customer segment is key, because after-sales service needs to be managed like sales service: based on customer segmentation and long-term profitability. Once again, high levels of commonality and low levels of complexity make it easier to plan for spares inventory management and returns.

Planning the physical network for spares is also key. In addition to manufacturing, stocking, and distributing spares, companies must plan for parts availability at service centers; management of returns, pickups, and packaging; location of major and minor repairs; and the logistics of returns. Figure 3.8 illustrates one such network concept for a major electronics manufacturer. Note the different operations performed at different stages.

Significant costs are often hidden in warranty tracking and recovery. Assume, for example, that a consumer buys a tape recorder that was assembled three weeks earlier. Most likely, several components are under warranty from various suppliers to the manufacturer. If the consumer returns the device—and the manufacturer hasn't tracked components by serial numbers, date of acquisition, and warranty duration— that manufacturer will probably:

➤ Lose the ability to make cost-effective decisions about repair versus replace, and who (supplier, manufacturer, or third party) should actually perform (or pay for) the work

➤ Shoulder 100 percent of the repair or replacement costs, without remuneration or consideration from the component supplier

➤ Fail to understand the genesis of the failure and, subsequently, to either plan for more failures or eliminate the problem

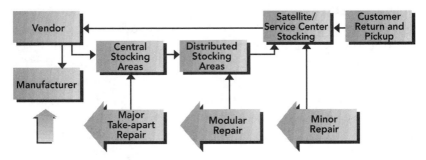

**Figure 3.8** Physical network management for spares and returns.

Finally, the process of customer segmentation even plays a role in spares and returns. Although warranty costs and procedures are likely to be consistent among all customer classes, *service lead times* are often segmentable. A supplier's commitments to its "A" customers probably means readily available service parts. Slower parts-ordering procedures may be more appropriate for narrow-margin "B" customers.

## ➤ 7. Replace Inventory with Information and Analysis

Excellent demand/supply management and planning will succeed in replacing inventory with information: real-time, accurate, and in a common format and language that is understandable across the enterprise. It should be no surprise, therefore, that demand/supply planning is data intensive. Neither managing that data—and transforming it into information for decision support and action—is ever easy, nor is obtaining the right mix of decision support functionality and intelligence, and implementing all this quickly so that managers (and, indeed, everyone inside and outside the enterprise) can use it all to good effect. However, no company should make this effort more difficult than it has to be.

Sourcing and implementing this information capability can be a complex undertaking, and adopting a simplistic approach can make it even more so. Too many divergent interests exist for the process to be anywhere close to simple. Beyond operational user interests, general market interests, and customer interests, there are also the interests of CIOs (which may not align with the first two), systems vendors (they need to sell and maintain a revenue stream), and senior executives (who want the best value for their money in terms of cost outlay, benefits, market flexibility, and speed to benefit). This variety of interests means that tough questions need to be asked. The harder, the better. Here are some examples.

### *What Is Our Base Information Technology Strategy?*

Are we opting for a single, one-size-fits-all system or several best-of-breed, smaller packages? Are our criteria comprehensive; that is, do they include increased throughput, faster cycle and response times, enhanced customer service, greater flexibility to operate in several channels and geographies, less working and fixed capital required, and lower operational costs? If these don't appear in the information systems strategy, then something is wrong (Figure 3.9).

A key component of information technology strategy is size. For example, integrated strings of smaller, best-in-class systems have several advantages over large, enterprise-wide, transaction-oriented systems (those that encompass every function within the company, including demand/supply). On balance, the former systems will be cheaper and quicker to install, easier to manage, more flexible, easier to troubleshoot, and easier to change as business conditions evolve or better applications emerge. Also, it is likely that smaller systems will better fit the needs of the business (or multiple businesses and channels). Moreover, because not all functionality becomes obsolete at the same time, these systems will last longer. Their modularity, size, and shape allow for piecemeal replacements, additions, and enhancements. One system may be viable for five years, whereas replacement of another can be justified after two or three years.

Large global systems, on the other hand, have the advantage of enforcing common terminology, product language, analysis parameters, and data; so they resolve many of the integration problems inherent in the multiple-systems environment. This is a significant advantage. Commonality makes it possible to perform analyses such as forecasting, demand planning, supply management, and optimization at different points and on different systems. It is also the key to capturing and communicating timely information among customers, suppliers, brokers, distributors, and logistics service providers. However, implementing complex

---

### OPERATIONAL INNOVATION: FROM PUSH TO PULL

**Airbus Industries** has migrated from a push to a pull system of manufacturing. This method of discontinuous manufacture has helped the company respond profitably to stiffer competition and rising expenses. By making only what the customer wants, when they need it, Airbus has been able to dramatically reduce manufacturing costs.*

*John Crampton, "Lean Manufacturing Is Just a Start," *Interavia Business & Technology*, 51, no. 602 (August 1996): 24–5.

---

monolithic systems requires an intimate knowledge of businesswide activities and future required processes. Few companies can do this; however—given today's high-flexibility, rapid-response business environment—not too many actually *need* it to a high level of detail.

Working with multiple applications, companies must make a basic business decision: Should their application systems be best of breed or quickest to implement? Having both is sometimes possible but always expensive. Regardless of the difficulties in making the choice, acquisition and implementation decisions should *never* default to acquiring one system for all functions and geographies, merely because such a move makes it easier for the company to work with a single vendor.

### What Is the Time to Implement? Will the Project Ever Be Completed?

There is no shortage of horror stories about perpetual implementations and astronomical cost overruns. Despite their causes, it is important to remember that large, enterprise-wide systems *are* expensive and *do* take a comparatively long time to implement. Also a strong likelihood exists that, by the time most companies are done implementing, their business justification and conditions will have changed to some extent. Moreover, newer systems may have emerged during the implementation cycle, thus giving competitors a potential advantage. On the other hand, implementing many smaller systems may be complex. This is why it is important that companies ascertain 1) whether the system they are considering has been successfully implemented *in a reasonable amount of time* by companies with similar operating characteristics (e.g., business units, geographies, facilities, supply chains, and channels), and 2) whether rapid implementation and enablement of your planning process could be achieved by using smaller, decision-support and point-solution systems—particularly leveraging the newer integration tools and capabilities available.

### *Who Is Driving the Decision, and What Is Their Primary Focus?*

The decision to acquire and implement supply chain systems is often driven by people with disparate goals. Sometimes, systems are pushed most heartily by functional managers seeking to better manage the complex details of their business units, markets, and channels. This is the way it *should* be: systems decisions driven by operational needs to understand costs, improve service, leverage capital, respond to customers, and increase competitiveness. Unfortunately, this doesn't happen often enough. More common are systems decisions driven by CFOs (e.g., to ensure common financial information) or CIOs (to reduce complexity for the IS department). These drivers invariably lead to the tail wagging the dog, and it is rarely fruitful. Another wrong reason is believing too strongly in the power of systems to solve supply chain problems. Systems, after all, are *enablers*. Developing, optimizing, and efficiently operating the supply chain requires a great deal more than chips n' bytes.

### Are You Buying or Being Sold To?

Is this the system you need? Will it help meet the operating plan? It is natural for systems vendors to move up the food chain, adding margin-enhancing functionality, cost, and complexity to their systems. However, to effectively run the supply chain, a lot of bells-and-whistles technology may not be needed. Also, too much complexity could easily make matters worse.

As they evolve toward increasingly operational systems (from their traditional bases of data transactions, financials, and human resource applications), many ERP systems purport to provide a complete suite of functions needed for decision support and management of a company's planning operations. Be sure, however, that you understand whether the vendor is selling you a line extension for your planning processes (moving downstream toward the higher-margin systems applications) and whether the increased functionality actually complements your business needs. Make sure that the vendor can define the minimum functionality needed to meet today's needs and provide the flexibility for tomorrow's. In our experience, the functionality of monolithic systems is not always a match for the independent (but integrable) decision-support and planning systems provided by smaller, more agile, and more focused companies.

### What Are You Paying? What Will You Pay?

Systems (in particular, *large* systems) can be extraordinarily expensive to acquire and implement. The total implementation cost will be several times the combined cost of hardware and software; moreover, precious IS and functional resources will be tied up for years. Therefore, before the decision is made, it is vital to understand the *real* cost of the effort:

➤ Hardware, software, and telecommunications costs
➤ IS department time to install and maintain the system

➤ Human resource costs to document business processes, functions, and develop scripts

➤ Time required of trainers and trainees

➤ External assistance, such as consultants, vendors, and subcontractors

➤ Opportunity costs

Armed with this knowledge, you can then decide if the company would be better off acquiring less expensive planning and decision support systems and using the rest of the cash to increase capacity, maintain working capital, or expand into new markets, geographies, or channels.

### What Benefits Will You Receive and When Will You Receive Them?

It's an unwritten law of business that projections about system benefits will be overly optimistic. The larger the system—and the more transaction oriented—the more likely this is to be true. It is not a reach, in fact, to say that transaction-focused systems *rarely* justify themselves within an acceptable time period. The fact that they provide commonality (e.g., of data and language) is a significant benefit, but with-

---

**OPERATIONAL INNOVATION: FROM PUSH TO PULL**

**Hewlett-Packard** has reengineered its factory logistics to cut cycle time and improve productivity. As part of the effort, the company implemented a pull manufacturing system: producing just what is actually needed instead of producing based on forecast. Higher productivity and lower production costs were among the benefits HP received.*

*James K. Allred, "New Direction," *IIE Solutions,* 28, no. 4 (April 1996): 21–5.

out improvements in delivery proficiency, supply-chain cost structure, or customer satisfaction, *real-cost justification* is unlikely. The tangible value proposition, in other words, is simply not there.

Cost-justifiable operational improvements are typically the by-product of systems that feature planning and decision support capabilities, for example, the ability to dynamically model supply chain activities. Despite their claims, many "soup-to-nuts" technology offerings focus primarily on transaction support. Therefore, functional (decision support) applications should not be thought of as extensions of transactional, data management systems. In most cases, data management and functional enhancement are vital, yet separate, issues.

### Does the System Have the Right Functionality for Demand/Supply Planning? Is It Comprehensive, Easy to Use, and Flexible?

For example, does the system (or integrated solution set of smaller systems) have sophisticated modeling and "what-if" capabilities that allow you to evaluate different demand/supply scenarios against the operating plan? Can it perform causal modeling of operations? Can it be used by several business units and geographies simultaneously? Is it workable across several different logistically separate businesses and channels? Does it allow for collaborative forecasting and replenishment with suppliers and customers? Can it plan for the entire spectrum of planning activities across the enterprise? Is it easy to set up and implement? These are questions that go beyond the obvious fit-functionality exercise that many companies do to select a demand/supply planning system.

Finally, like EMV-focused supply chains, effective demand/supply planning systems will push *and* pull. Financial targets, supply positions, inventory constraints, and excesses are pushed through to the customer. Conversely, POS, order, and

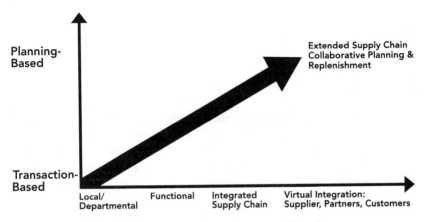

**Figure 3.9** Moving from transaction and local systems to planning-based, multienterprise systems.

consumption data generate a customer-specific replenishment pattern. A good planning system will capture POS data; connect with MRPII/DRPII systems all the way to the supplier; and provide on-line information about inventory, orders, supply position, and other supply chain events. Once again, the key is *integration of common data.*

## ➤ 8. Focus on Transparency in Planning and Deployment

In today's world, the company that makes a product is unlikely to be the one that sells it, delivers it, services it, or finances it. Sometimes—in this age of the virtual corporation—the company doesn't even make the product. However, the company with the name on the box is still the one that will lose business if any link in the chain fails.

This hard reality explains why transparency is so important to today's manufacturers. To ensure market growth and customer retention, no handoff can place an additional burden on the customer. Customers must see a single face, a single point of contact, a single supply chain. Failure to present

## CONTINUOUS REPLENISHMENT: REPLACING INVENTORY WITH INFORMATION

Continuous replenishment is a practice and process that exemplifies the role integrated information (and information sharing) plays in demand/supply planning. Continuous replenishment encompasses the complete inventory cycle, including returns. Relationships with suppliers, customers, asset/logistics providers, brokers, distributors, and inventory managers must reflect this. Continuous replenishment is also highly information intensive. It is usage and consumption triggered (e.g., through POS data); statistically backed (analysis based on consumption data); and enabled by the implementation of vendor-managed and comanaged inventory processes. Because it is so information intensive, it must be tightly coupled with high-cost, high-redundancy areas, such as fixed capital, working capital, storage, picking and stocking, excess and damage, handling, accounting for inventory damage, and freight.

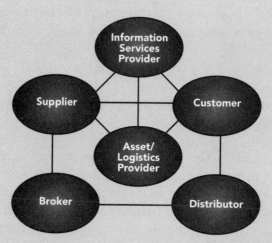

**Continuous replenishment information and partnerships must be supply chain wide and encompass the complete inventory cycle.**

*(Continued)*

Continuous replenishment illustrates the basic supply chain principal of replacing inventory with information—not only obvious information like purchase orders and stock levels, but also information from:

➤ Asset providers (about distribution capacity)

➤ Brokers (about what's on the road)

➤ Freight providers (about status of activities, such as merge in transit or merge at customer dock)

➤ Distributors (about replenishment/restocking issues)

After all, information is cheaper and easier to manipulate than inventory. The more accurate information that can be provided and managed along the supply chain, the more improvements will be observed in response time, customer satisfaction, customer targeting, working capital, fixed capital reductions, and cost reduction.

that face translates into lost business for the manufacturer, both in customer acquisition *and* retention. Excuses don't fly. Customers simply have too many choices, and they don't really care if it is one integrated supply chain or a series of supply chains working together that delivers their products at the right prices and times.

Integrated demand/supply planning is one key to achieving transparency: linking the different supply chains and managing the handoffs among suppliers, manufacturers, distributors, transportation providers, and other business partners, as well as other business units. If a customer desires a software upgrade from the hardware company that installed its old software, then the demand-planning cycle must comprehend that—in manufacturing, in inventory, in third-party logistics providers, and in service. Demand/supply planning is the window through which the complete supply chain must be visible: the entire material flow—from the first supplier to the customer *and back*—as well as all parties in between. It is the glue that convinces customers that one seamless supply chain is working to take and fulfill their orders, and it is the key to effective, flexible, and cost-competitive operations.

## ■ SUMMARY

Demand/supply management is one of the few functions in the company that must be enterprise wide and credentialized by senior management. It should extend, as appropriate, to key suppliers and customers, as well as to all major functions within the company: from new product development, to operations and finance, to sales and marketing.

Demand/supply management drives working capital investment, fixed capital utilization, supplier planning, overall tax minimization, and customer service. It deserves the attention of (and management by) a company's best and brightest. In short, it is the driver of the operating plan and must be measured as such.

---

### ASK YOUR MANAGERS

➤ Are the right business areas actively involved in demand/supply planning?

➤ How is the demand/supply planning process measured? Who is directly responsible?

➤ Are key suppliers and customers involved in the planning process?

➤ Are there meaningful metrics tied directly to the operating plan projections and results?

➤ Is the demand/supply plan being actively managed on a weekly basis?

➤ Is the process enabled by the best tools and systems?

➤ Are the data accurate?

➤ Who is the senior executive ultimately responsible?

# Selling More: Winning the Customer with Operational Excellence

Most companies would agree that *maximizing enterprise market value* is their preeminent goal. Also, they would concur that operational excellence cannot be the singular strategy for achieving it. To some extent, this is true. Operating at minimum cost and maximum efficiency produces business benefits that are real, but not organizationally comprehensive. Nevertheless, businesses consistently undervalue the contribution that operational excellence (i.e., supply chain management) *does* make to growing the customer base: to successfully creating/entering new markets and taking market share from competitors. This chapter discusses how superior supply chain management can help companies create and enter new markets and enhance revenues. It is built around three core beliefs:

➤ Effective supply chain management has as much to do with revenue growth as it does with cost control.

➤ Channel focus is as important as customer focus.

➤ All customers are not created equal.

## ■ CONNECTING CORPORATE GROWTH TO THE SUPPLY CHAIN

For most companies, the traditional relationship between supply chain management and cost containment is clear. In fact, logistical innovations are at the core of many companies' most dramatic gains in efficiency. But what about profitable growth: the real source of increased EMV? What can supply chain management contribute to the successful penetration of new markets? . . . to the attainment of competitive advantage? . . . to the profitable expansion of global business?

This issue will become even more important in the near future, as greater levels of parity are reached in best practice knowledge, system quality, and incremental improvement. As a result, differentiation that is based on these three measures will become exceptionally difficult to achieve. After all, virtually all companies are fixated on best practices, are all copying the same group of leaders, and all are adopting similar information technologies to help plan, buy, make, and move their products.

> "Delighted customers do not automatically produce delighted shareholders."

Executives at many companies believe they know the answer: service-intensive, "pull" supply chains that are stimulated solely by market demand. Clearly, being hyperresponsive to customer demands has merit. However, all-pull operations—in addition to being economically unrealistic—are far more difficult to implement than their production-driven "push" predecessors. And the key characteristics of today's marketplace—high fragmentation, more channels, and rapid proliferation of products and technologies—only make it worse. It should come as no surprise, therefore, when companies discover that delighted customers do not automatically produce delighted shareholders. This is why businesses actually need a dual "customer-centric, supply-aware"

---

**OPERATIONAL INNOVATION:**
**ONE-TO-ONE MARKETING**

**Sears, Roebuck and Company** uses data warehouse technology to get closer to its customers. Sears relies on its Strategic Performance Reporting System (SPRS) as the authoritative and single source for sales, margin, and inventory data for the retail business. Since implementing the new system, Sears has enjoyed lower operating costs, increased sales, and more frequent inventory turns.*

*Renee Covino Kruger, "Are We Pushing the Right Buttons?," *Discount Merchandiser*, 37, no. 2 (February 1997): 58–63.

---

philosophy of operation. The tenets of this fiscally responsible (push-pull) approach include:

➤ Reconciling demand with supply constraints and opportunities

➤ Emphasizing profitability by channel, product, and customer

➤ Identifying the value contributed by each business function

Marching in lock step with a balanced push-pull system is the concept of *differentiation through service value:* leveraging supply chain flexibility to grow profits. After all, delighting, satisfying, obsessing about, or even establishing intimacy with customers says nothing about a company's ability to successfully create value for itself. Thus, the missing link between supply chain (operational) expertise and profitable growth is *differentiated service.* Companies with the link firmly in place can charge higher prices because of the enhanced service value of their products. Most enjoy larger margins, higher share, and stronger growth.

So why have few companies successfully made the connection? Perhaps it is because they are not convinced that differentiation through service can be profitable (or workable). However, the reality is that superior, yet differentiated, customer service is not only profitable, it should also be universally desirable! This doesn't mean that companies should create such a presence in all service segments or across all channels. But it does mean that differentiation within a carefully chosen service arena is more and more key to harnessing and maintaining competitive advantage. This is the concept of bundles: channel-specific product/service combinations developed to differentiate through service value.

## ■ SALES AND MARKETING: GATEWAY TO THE NEW SUPPLY CHAIN

Customer-centered companies work harder to create customer value. And their supply chain management processes are always aligned with—and fully accountable to—the company's defined business needs, especially those focused on profitable growth. For them, operational excellence and growth accrues by carefully aligning operations with the sales and marketing strategies of the firm.

As always, customer focus begins with sales and marketing. We know that as more and more products assume generic characteristics, the more differentiation and customer value become associated with service. It is also true that the more global a company's reach becomes, the more its success hinges on delivery. Forward-thinking organizations build that reality into their sales and marketing strategies. That is, they place greater strategic emphasis on aligning operations with sales and marketing.

The new business model for selling product focuses more on delighting customers with a great "experience" than satisfying them with a differentiated product or service. Good examples abound in the automobile industry: Making car-buying a customer-friendly experience is paying off for Saturn, as well as for new players such as CarMax. Putting yourself in the customer's shoes and then redesigning the *buying process* (not the

> ## OPERATIONAL INNOVATION: ONE-TO-ONE MARKETING
>
> **Procter & Gamble Co.** and **Wal-Mart Stores, Inc.** have had a "relationship marketing" partnership for years. Within this arrangement, P&G manages certain product lines in Wal-Mart's inventory and decides when to deliver its shipments. Procter & Gamble has complete information access to Wal-Mart's inventory, as well as to sales data. This approach has helped Wal-Mart to reduce operating costs and made it possible for P&G to increase market share.*
>
> *Vincent Alonzo, "'Til Death Do Us Part," *Incentive*, 168, no. 4 (April 1994): 37–42.

selling process) is one key to future business success. This is the secret of developing differentiated, target bundles.

In the good old days, companies could reach all of their customers through traditional sales channels. Many times, they could use one channel, such as a chain of stores. But today, and well into the future, new channel creation will be the norm. Consider electronic commerce. We once thought that the Internet would be an interesting way to browse, but not to buy. Yet shopping on the Internet—the full transaction from buying to receiving to paying—is increasing at a rate of 50 percent every quarter. The net effect is that most manufacturers now sell through mass merchants, wholesalers, specialty retailers, and direct-to-consumer channels. Each one of these requires a discrete marketing and supply chain strategy.

Even today, most sales force models still focus on the end user—the terminus of the single-customer supply chain. These approaches ignore the fact that, in addition to myriad channels, most supply chains have customers at multiple intersect points and that each of them contributes (and expects) added value. Thus, modern supply chain thinking requires marketers to identify and optimize each of these prospective value points. (See Figure 4.1.)

As mentioned earlier, the most important shift to which marketers must react is the changing balance between push and pull. All along the supply chain, customers have more power. Their increased control of quantities, characteristics, delivery modes, and delivery times means that "sell" drives the supply chain paradigm. *Buy-make-move-sell* is now *sell-buy-make-move*. Moreover, because the pull is exerted along many channels, supply chain decision makers risk losing control over process as well as over content. End to end, companies must rebalance their operations to become demand driven *and* supply aware.

To abet the transition, traditional sales force models must be retired, with new sales and marketing organizations built around channels. Marketers—like companies—must become more profitably market driven. (See Figure 4.2.)

## ➤ Addressing the New Marketplace: One-to-One

Despite current trends, most markets follow a consistent evolutionary path. They rise from highly fragmented popula-

| Today | Tomorrow | Supply Chain Implications |
|---|---|---|
| Market share via head-on battles | Market share and profits via niches | Tailored services |
| National media campaigns through few channels | Targeted regional campaigns through multimedia | Tailored services |
| Look-alike products and services | Customized products and services | Differentiated channels and product/service bundles |
| Numerous transactional relations | Strategic partners | Strategic management |
| Creativity around a message | Creativity around a customer | Flexibility and responsiveness |
| Mass marketing | Niche marketing | Niche chains |
| Pushing cases | Pulling choices | Virtual responses |

**Figure 4.1** Marketing trends.

| Sales Driven (Old) | Market Driven (New) |
|---|---|
| ➤ Market manipulation (push) | ➤ More customer need-centered and supply-aware (pull-push) |
| ➤ Sales and margins | ➤ Balanced scorecard (ROI, sales, margins, customer satisfaction) |
| ➤ Efficiency and scale | ➤ Flexibility and responsiveness |
| ➤ Product centered | ➤ Value-added services centered bundles |
| ➤ Mass production | ➤ Mass customization |
| ➤ Make and sell offerings | ➤ Market response driven |
| ➤ Promotion | ➤ Benefits and value selling |
| ➤ Little accountability, multiple contacts | ➤ Empowered single point of contact |
| ➤ Knowledge and information are controlled | ➤ Knowledge and information are shared |
| ➤ One-time transaction | ➤ Ongoing relationship/customer franchise management |
| ➤ Customers at end of the process | ➤ Customers integrated into the process |

**Figure 4.2** Implications of a market-driven focus.

tions that know few product differences. Mass-marketing strategies come later as markets coalesce, but product differentiation remains low. This is the marketing venue of commodities. Next comes micro- or niche marketing, in which markets are largely unfragmented, but products are increasingly differentiated. The final frontier—much of which is occurring today—is high market fragmentation and high product differentiation. This is often referred to as *one-to-one marketing* (Figure 4.3).

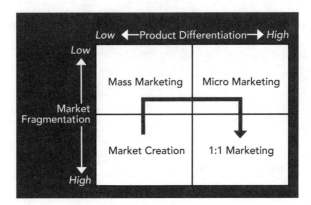

**Figure 4.3** The marketing matrix.

One-to-one marketing is a different kind of marketing process. It teams with customers to increase customer share. It demands that companies be managers of customer portfolios, rather than managers of brands and products. Most important, one-to-one marketing acknowledges (and even exploits) fragmentation throughout the supply chain: multiple customers (e.g., the trade and end users), multiple market types (e.g., mature versus emerging), multiple channels, and multiple geographies (e.g., local, national, global).

In addition, one-to-one marketing responds to the reality of too many products chasing too little shelf space and too few consumers. The more products proliferate, the more suppliers must tighten their market focus. In mature markets, for example, nearly everyone buys deodorant; so marketing and supply chain strategies at the trade and consumer level aim to expand specific customer niches at the expense of competitors. In emerging markets, however, not everyone uses deodorant. Thus, consumer marketers focus more on the generic need for deodorant, even as trade marketing aims to improve service and differentiate between brands.

One-to-one marketing also has its genesis in two other events. The first is new media and channel options. Electronic commerce, interactive TV, the Internet, electronic kiosks, interactive CD catalogs, home shopping, and niche

---

**OPERATIONAL INNOVATION:
CHANNEL AND PRODUCT
DIFFERENTIATION**

**Sherwin-Williams Co.** has increased market share by using a strategy known as brand tiering. This approach involves stratifying brands by price point, segment, and/or channel. For example, the company sells its own Sherwin-Williams brand at company-owned stores, whereas second brands such as Kem-Tone are sold to discounters. Brand-labeled products like Easy-Living and Weatherbeater are sold to Sears as exclusive, private-label paints.*

*Allan J. Magrath, "Where It's at in Branding," *Business Quarterly,* 61, no. 3 (Spring 1997): 65–70.

---

retailers have fragmented the marketplace, forcing manufacturers to identify new points of differentiation. What's more, the same technologies that spawned many of these options have also helped to commoditize products. For example, the sheer availability of information (e.g., through the Internet or 500-channel satellite TV) reduces brand loyalty by making data on price, performance, and alternatives more available to consumers, thereby allowing easier comparisons along multiple dimensions. The net effect of these influences is that from 1960 to 2000, share of consumers' dollars focused on traditional retail channels will have shrunk by nearly one-half. Better marketing and stronger differentiation are survival mechanisms.

The second one-to-one marketing event is a shift in customer priorities. Whereas price used to be key, many surveys show that in the U.S., service, quality, and selection now rank higher than purchase price. The message is that more and more customers are changing and upgrading their perspectives on value. The typical consumer in the developed world is better educated, more sophisticated, more time constrained, and more expectant of treatment that meets his or her unique needs and preferences. Successful manufacturers will respond with specific value bundles encompassing tailored, value-added services, customized products, and high levels of understanding about the consumer. This is the basis of one-to-one marketing. The roots of one-to-one marketing lie in:

- ➤ Market fragmentation
- ➤ Product proliferation
- ➤ New media and channel options
- ➤ Shifting consumer priorities
- ➤ Technology power

It is also true, however, that consumer priorities vary significantly among global regions and often from country to country. In Latin America—a burgeoning market for many manufacturers—price remains paramount. The same is typically true in most poorer countries and many emerging markets. Thus, companies' supply chain strategies must acknowledge the trade-offs that exist among different markets and regions (e.g., lower price versus better service). See Figure 4.4.

## ■ SALES AND MARKETING MEETS SUPPLY CHAIN MANAGEMENT

In customer-focused companies, sales and marketing and supply chain expertise come together to address market fragmentation, product proliferation/saturation, new media/channel options, and shifting consumer priorities. Supply chain capabilities help define global marketing strategy, because it is along the supply chain that most cost and service advantage can be gained or lost. In other words, sales and marketing efforts that *successfully* address highly fragmented markets with differentiated products/services will be those with the supply chain expertise needed to strategize and execute consistently. Conversely, those with supply

| Value Chain Element | Traditional Themes | Innovation Themes |
|---|---|---|
| Customer life-cycle management | ➤ Market share<br>➤ Transaction<br>➤ Short-term profits | ➤ Lifetime share of customer/consumer<br>➤ Collaboration<br>➤ Customer retention |
| Products and services | ➤ Efficiency/ predictability<br><br><br>➤ Mass production | ➤ Flexibility and responsiveness<br>➤ Tailored product/ service/price bundles<br>➤ Mass customization/postponement |
| Integrated supply chain | ➤ Customers at the end of the process | ➤ Customers integrated into the process |
| Pricing and promotion | ➤ Mass marketing and promotion<br>➤ Economies of scale | ➤ Marketing tailored one customer at a time<br>➤ Economies of scope |
| Customer service and after-sales support | ➤ Customer calls with a problem<br>➤ Sales and marketing | ➤ Problems diagnosed and fixed without customer awareness<br>➤ Consumer management (single point of contact) |

**Figure 4.4** Elements of the one-to-one marketing value chain.

chain inefficiencies will yield ground previously gained through effective marketing. Account management and consumer direct marketing are two new areas in which supply chain management intersects with one-to-one marketing.

Within the one-to-one marketing model, an account management approach can effectively leverage a company's supply chain capabilities. More and more companies are redefining sales and marketing as account management, and one of the key differences is how effectively service is leveraged as a selling tool. Thus, account management combines leading-edge technology and business practices with supply chain capabilities to build service programs that meet specific needs of specific customers—one-to-one! These programs can be applied with equal effectiveness in build-to-order as well as the more traditional build-to-forecast (push) environments. The key is who you're selling to and how well you deliver. (See Figure 4.5.)

In an account management framework, account managers serve as single points of contact for products and value-added services. They are also a conduit for real-time information exchange throughout the value chain, and they are the most important virtual link between supplier and customer or between supplier and consumer.

The second intersect point is consumer-direct marketing. As companies become more proficient in one-to-one marketing, they naturally seek more direct selling (and service) channels. A consumer-direct channel builds on one-to-one profiles developed for individual consumers. Similar to other applications of one-to-one thinking, the objective is to obtain the largest share of the best consumers' spending on products and services by anticipating their needs and offering convenient, responsive, one-stop shopping and support.

Development of a one-to-one consumer program requires ongoing dialogue between the supplier and each individual consumer, so that the supplier's knowledge of that consumer

---

### OPERATIONAL INNOVATION: CONSUMER-DIRECT MARKETING

**Dell Computer Corp.** pioneered direct marketing in its industry. Dell sells its custom-built PCs directly to consumers. As a result, the company enjoys low operating costs and 12 to 15 days of inventory, compared with the industry norm of six to eight weeks.*

*Lesley Meall, "Are You Being Served?," *Accountancy*, 117, no. 1231 (March 1996): 48–9.

| Account Management Recognizes Specific Customer Demands for: | Account Management Responds to General Market Requirements to: |
| --- | --- |
| ➤ Direct distribution<br>➤ Real-time product availability<br>➤ Merchandising support closer to the end consumer<br>➤ A single point of contact | ➤ Support multiple channels<br>➤ Support multiple product configurations<br>➤ Concurrently support multiple locations and geographies |

| Account Management Is Key to Adding Customer Value by: | Account Management's Documented Benefits Include: |
| --- | --- |
| ➤ Accommodating special orders<br>➤ Increasing customer face time<br>➤ Creating tailored services approaches<br>➤ Helping customers be more successful<br>➤ Enhancing differentiation | ➤ Sales increases<br>➤ Sell-through sales lifts<br>➤ Operational cost reductions<br>➤ Shorter cycle times for account penetration |

**Figure 4.5** Account management is an effective response to growing customer power and focus.

*"Once the cost-reduction ceiling has been reached, all companies need to sell more, not cut more. They need to focus on revenue and profits, not just on cost savings."*

exceeds that of its competitors (Figure 4.6). Consumers must have an incentive to engage in this one-to-one dialogue initially (e.g., frequent-flyer programs). Mail-order fulfillment companies are today's most advanced consumer-direct marketers.

Within the consumer-direct model, product managers and marketing managers may eventually give way to consumer or customer managers. Consumer managers will estimate consumer lifetime value and then work with each customer or consumer to reach or exceed that value. Channels will evolve many times as we move into the next decade. During this period of change, establishing one-to-one relationships with end consumers will differentiate many successful suppliers from the also-rans.

Clearly, marketing and supply chain trends point to a narrower, yet more diverse, marketing focus. Today's performance goals quickly become tomorrow's expectations. Quality, efficiency, and manufacturing economy evolve from luxuries into entitlements, and in the process lose their ability to create differentiation. Replacing them are more service-oriented themes with renewed differentiation potential such

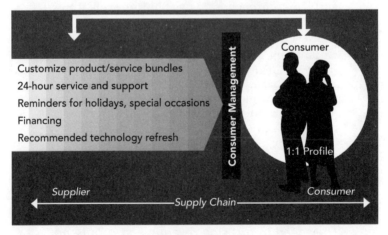

**Figure 4.6** Customer needs are the key determinant of supplier value-added services.

as flexibility, responsiveness, and mass customization. Within these new models, customers kick-start the process. One-to-one marketing, account management, and consumer-direct marketing help companies cater to these new customers. In so doing, they learn to penetrate accounts more completely, expand market share, expand channels effectively, and get closer to all customers.

## ■ A NEW CUSTOMER SATISFACTION LEXICON

Sales and marketing is tasked with connecting with the new customer. Supply chain management is the enabling process. We have observed that innovative sales and marketing programs—integrated with creative supply chains—are yielding sales increases of 10 to 40 percent, sell-through sales increases of 50 percent and more, and significant operational cost reductions. Linking the new marketing imperatives with supply chain innovation requires companies to think differently about customer service, customer satisfaction, and customer value: the three categories of customer focus.

Start with *service*. The dictionary describes it as "an act of assistance or benefit to another or others" and "work done for others." Missing is the critical notion of added value, which is increasingly essential in a business environment where more and more products are perceived as generic, brand loyalty is eroding, and price and quality are less effective differentiators. Therefore, companies must first adopt a broader perspective of customer service as

> . . . the process that takes place between buyers, sellers, and third parties that results in value added to the product or service exchanged. This process involves short-term and long-term transactions (as the result of a contractual relationship or a relationship based on mutual benefit).

Value-focused customer service produces benefits beyond those achievable through product-based differentiation (see Figure 4.7):

➤ Opportunity to become a preferred supplier

➤ Increased sales and share gains

➤ Business stability during periods of slower product growth

➤ Volume protection as new products decline

➤ Opportunities for cost reduction programs (pipeline inventories and lead time reduction)

➤ Merchandising advantages at the point of sale

Next, *customer satisfaction*—the user's contentedness with products or services—must also take on new meaning. Like service, satisfaction is increasingly a function of value. Benchmarks such as "did it arrive on time?" or "was the product defect-free?" are less meaningful, because they aspire to avoid losing value rather than capturing additional value. They are also supplier defined, that is, they use supplier-generated benchmarks instead of those determined by the customer.

| Pretransaction | Transaction | | Posttransaction |
|---|---|---|---|
| ➤ Policies | ➤ Order cycle times | ➤ Communication | ➤ Information |
| ➤ Organization | ➤ Reliability | ➤ Delivery lead time | ➤ Claims, returns |
| ➤ Flexibility | ➤ Accuracy | ➤ Delivery quality | ➤ Tracking |
| ➤ Technical services | ➤ Completeness | ➤ Delivery flexibility and response | ➤ After-sales service |
| ➤ Practices | ➤ Convenience | ➤ Ease of information access | |

**Figure 4.7** Elements of value-focused customer service.

Consider surveys that ask drivers about their *satisfaction.* (See Figure 4.8.) Luxury car owners typically rate their cars extremely high: "good product," "drives well," "good ergonomics." Yet only one-third of highly satisfied owners of luxury cars buy the same model or brand a second time. What does this say about satisfaction? For one thing, it says that the connection between customer satisfaction and customer loyalty is either broken or nonexistent. To be relevant today, satisfaction must focus on the relationship, and it must use customer-defined benchmarks. What, in other words, must the supplier do to earn the customer's loyalty and to cement the relationship? Given these parameters, think of customer satisfaction as

> . . . the overall view or perspective that customers have regarding the suppliers of a particular product or service or product/service bundle. Their views may be based on tangible elements (quality, reliability, transactions) or on intangibles (behavior, information, helpfulness). Usually both are involved.

Finally, *customer value* says that effective service—as well as effective satisfaction measures—must focus on improving the convenience of performance of the customer. To leverage service as a competitive tool, the transaction must contribute value. Preferred suppliers know that their service activities have to *benefit* their customers, not simply satisfy them. They define customer value as

> . . . the degree to which the provider of a product/service goes beyond customer requirements/expectations to enhance customer performance; the result of which should be mutual benefits to both provider and customer.

In a traditional transaction, for example, the customer might submit an order with instructions to fill it in five days. Within five days, the order is filled. The transaction is completed. The customer is satisfied. However, it costs the cus-

| Meaningful Customer Satisfaction Assessments Should: | Customer Satisfaction Self-Questionnaire: |
|---|---|
| ➤ Emphasize data that are measurable.<br>➤ Evaluate the supplier as closely as the product.<br>➤ Highlight the quality of the supplier/customer relationship.<br>➤ Focus on issues that are relevant to the customer, for example, use primarily customer-generated benchmarks.<br>➤ Factor in the customer's expectations.<br>➤ Provide feedback to product, service, and supply chain design. | ➤ Are service policies and practices linked to the business strategy?<br>➤ Do we segment our market and tailor services to customers? Do we have the right bundles?<br>➤ How do our customers evaluate us?<br>➤ Are we predictable and consistent?<br>➤ Do we continuously review and refine our practices?<br>➤ Do we retain or lose customers? How? Why?<br>➤ Are we a customer-centered company?<br>➤ Are we moving beyond satisfying customer requirements and into enhancing customer performance? |

**Figure 4.8** Customer satisfaction assessments and key questions.

tomer a certain amount to make an order. It costs the supplier a certain amount to process, ship, and bill the order. Also, it costs the customer a certain amount to pay the bill. Customer value says that supplier and customer should work together to reduce those costs, perhaps through paperless transactions, or perhaps through vendor-managed inventories. Goods are delivered correctly and on time for less overall cost. Value is added.

*What makes the customer value concept work is innovative supply chain management.* Next, we look at how suppliers can create an atmosphere in which supply chain management can be leveraged to create simultaneous and consistent benefit for all participants.

# ■ CUSTOMER VALUE STRATEGIES

After years of downsizing, rightsizing, and exorcising, many companies have a cost-reduction hangover—the headache you get from waking up to the fact that cost-effective operations alone don't generate growth. (Plus, the costs seem to return, somehow.) Cost effectiveness can enable and enhance growth; but sustainable, profitable growth is still a function of expanding share and capturing new markets while retaining existing ones. Once the cost-reduction ceiling has been reached, all companies need to sell more, not cut more. They need to focus on revenue and profits, not just on cost savings. The secret to both is putting value into relationships rather than focusing exclusively on taking costs out.

But what is value anyway? The term has always been loosely defined and even more loosely applied. Fortunately, reaching consensus on a definition is less important than building an environment of *value management:* identifying ways that suppliers and customers can benefit from long-term, mutually sustaining collaborations. Unfortunately, most supply chain managers do not think in these terms. Their focus is usually on discrete benchmarks, such as order fill rates and on-time deliveries, rather than on how to creatively improve customers' performance. Also, many supply chain managers simply do not know enough about their customers' businesses to think in strategic terms. Whatever the reason, added value must be actively sought throughout the supply chain. No other process has so much potential to derive increased benefit through the delivery of products, services, and information.

Procter & Gamble and Wal-Mart comprise one of the most widely known supplier-customer collaborations. Focused on comanaging inventory, this partnership rests on the proposition that P&G brings extra value to Wal-Mart by keeping this key customer proactively supplied with the right amount of product, at the right place, at the right time, and in the right quantities—with as little clerical activity as possible. Since the partnership's inception, creative business managers at both companies have sought to exceed—indeed, alter—the traditional elements of customer service. Widely publicized, the results have raised the value-proposition bar across all industries.

For P&G, Wal-Mart, and virtually all companies, enterprise value is created through lasting improvements in one or more of five categories:

➤ Revenue growth: increase sales.

➤ Cost reductions: reduce operating costs.

➤ Working capital: decrease capital tied up in liquid assets (e.g., inventory).

➤ Fixed capital: minimize capital tied up in fixed assets (e.g., facilities).

➤ Tax minimization: cut effective tax rates.

Improvement in each or most of these categories can result from an interenterprise effort to combine supply chain expertise with higher levels of customer knowledge and insight. No business issue should be more important to senior operating executives, because nowhere are there greater opportunities for long-term benefit and sustained competitive advantage. Moreover, today's marketplace contains unprecedented value-creation opportunities. Customers expect more product styling and quality; merchandising support; customized fulfillment and delivery; industry expertise; higher inventory productivity; and strategic assistance. As a result, suppliers have more choices about how to build new value into their relationships—to create growth-focused differentiation strategies that reach their bottom line, as well as the bottom lines of their customers. The key is selection: wrapping the right few value disciplines around the right capabilities, the right markets, and the right customers. No company, after all, can hope to dominate on all customer value dimensions. Nor should most companies offer premium, value-added service to all customers. This emphasis on stratification is where supply chain management meets *the new marketing*: fragmented markets—each with unique requirements and profitability profiles—are contacted and served in unique, yet efficient ways.

---

*"In the new marketing, fragmented markets—each with unique requirements and profitability profiles—are contacted and served in unique, yet efficient ways."*

---

The preamble to sell-buy-make-move is a four-stage strategy for planning and implementing profitable, differentiated service. It focuses on segmenting markets, making customer value choices (creating targeted product/service bundles), consolidating (redundant or nonvalue adding) supply chains, and developing common processes and systems. From the outset, it is important to acknowledge that cost and service leadership are not mutually exclusive. High-quality, differentiated service—built on superior market knowledge and supply chain excellence—can produce consistent increases in growth and EMV. Here are four key steps to value-focused supply chain success.

## ➤ 1. Segment Markets and Product Groups

Virtually all companies do some type of market segmentation. They target marketing messages for discrete products to discrete groups. Some build supply chain approaches around market and product characteristics, and structure distinct manufacturing, transportation, and distribution approaches based on demand profiles. Yet few companies develop segmentation approaches that help them ascertain where and how to elevate customer value. Still fewer companies develop segmentation approaches that take full advantage of the enormous data/information available on customers and consumers to create value-added bundles.

The most important component of innovative segmentation strategies is the process into which new ideas can fit. Traditional segmentation methods—often driven by statistics or demographics—are still necessary but no longer sufficient (Figure 4.9). What must be adopted is a new way of approaching segmentation that drives *value,* not categorization. The P&G/Wal-Mart partnership was initiated (and is sustained) on this basis.

In global markets, although the same principles apply, implementation may vary depending on the types of markets, relative competition, product line, supply chain channels, and nature of the industry. The PC industry provides a useful example. Although the market has matured rapidly in the United States, and somewhat in Europe, emerging markets are quite another story. Yet creative segmenting of customers may expose new business opportunities—such as Michael Dell saw when he introduced consumer-direct sales and deliveries into Asian markets that, heretofore, relied

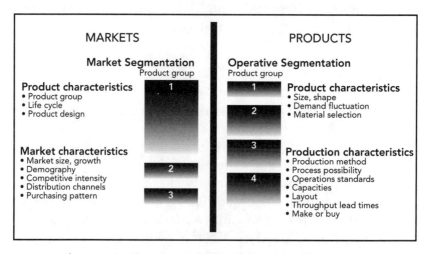

**Figure 4.9** The segmentation approach: disaggregating markets and products for focus.

only on traditional channels. (Note: Chapters 2 and 3 contain additional information on segmentation.)

## ➤ 2. Identify Key Value Points by Customer

Ask yourself: For each of my key customers, what elements of service would add the most value to their business? Myriad options exist, such as:

- ➤ Reducing their costs in overhead, assets, and planning
- ➤ Category management
- ➤ Joint distribution/logistics
- ➤ Best practice sharing
- ➤ Collaborative planning
- ➤ Joint promotions
- ➤ Joint product development
- ➤ Strategic alliances
- ➤ New creative solutions

Identifying and implementing the right service element(s) means aligning each customer's principal service need(s) with the supply chain expertise you possess (or can build) to make it happen. Of course, no company can possibly deliver value-added service to all customers across all channels and markets. This is why segmentation is needed to tailor or customize value programs.

Again, an example from the PC industry serves to reinforce this point. Figure 4.10 illustrates how one company decided to focus on excellence in order fulfillment as a differentiator in the midst of intense rivalry and relative product parity. The key value proposition was that, as buying criteria, customer satisfaction and value became more important as product commoditization became more prevalent. Dell, Hewlett-Packard, and Compaq, especially, have

**Potential Entrants**
- Alliance players are entering the market
- Entering organizations are large companies
- Entrants are attacking the direct market
- Little product differentiation exists
- Entrants are attacking existing channels

**Supplier Power**
- Limited suppliers for PC components
- Alliances are being formed with suppliers to facilitate development
- Suppliers drive technology and price

**Substitute Products**
- No viable substitutes for PCs

PC Industry

**Buyer Power**
- Several viable competitors increase buyer power
- Product parity allows for product switching for second-time buyers

**Rivalry Among Competitors**
- Intensifying as product increases commodity attributes
- Heavy price competition
- Widespread product and service copying
- Slow market growth expected

**Competitive Challenges for Order Fulfillment**

- Reduce order-processing costs to protect profits as prices fall
- Develop internal operations (order handling) that are transparent to the consumer
- Use service to differentiate as product parity increases
- Create buyer loyalty with an easy, accurate order-fulfillment process

**Figure 4.10** Intense rivalries and product parity increase the need to differentiate via order fulfillment.

proven this to be true. Their shareholder value (and stock price) growth can be traced directly to operational excellence, both internally and with their key customer accounts.

Another critical differentiator in today's high-tech industries is after-sales support. Technology alone will not do it anymore, and almost everyone now produces in the same low-cost regions of the world. Whereas American customers tend to be seen as more demanding (in terms of time) than most others, the worldwide reality is that it is fast becoming unacceptable to provide slower service to non-U.S. markets. Even emerging-market customers are getting acquainted with the concept of service value, and as customer expectations rise, suppliers must provide superb service around the globe.

As competitors raise the bar in after-sales service, however, suppliers are faced with the realities of cost, the value of loyalty, and often, whether to outsource the process itself. Some studies reveal that it costs up to ten times more to lose a customer than to retain one. If this is the case, why don't companies work harder to build and sustain loyalty and, thus, retain customers?

The answer lies in the ability to design and operate supply chains in a customer-centered manner. This principle means that regardless of where we operate globally, our supply chain processes and information systems are organized around, and focus on, common approaches to customer value. Customers may differ according to whether they are global, regional, or local; however, world-class supply chains organize, plan, and deliver on the universal basis of *what customers value.*

---

*"World-class supply chains organize, plan, and deliver on the basis of what customers value."*

---

Another key differentiator in certain industries and markets is *customer interaction systems:* technologies that facilitate communications—and value—between suppliers and customers. Motorola, for example, has developed software that lets customers jump-start their use of products and, thus, minimize the need for technical assistance. And Microsoft has installed customer service software that enables support engineers to immediately help a customer caller by providing real-time information about the customer's current systems configuration.

A final value point concerns customer partnerships. It is difficult, if not impossible, to succeed with customer value programs without some type of partnership—largely because insight is derived only from knowledge, and knowledge comes from collaboration. For individual consumers, this partnership is more explicit: it is based on loyalty and mutual benefit and driven by the suppliers' understanding of the customer's preferences and buying patterns. When supplier-customer teams are established, learning occurs and improvement opportunities are identified. This is not to suggest that full partnerships are always required for customer value management. Indeed, there are several levels possible in a relationship, but it is important that managers agree to work together for win-win value propositions.

## ➤ 3. Identify Consolidation Opportunities around the Customer

When evaluating their supply chains, many companies discover that separate chains often exist for certain products—in some cases, flowing to the same customer account. This is especially true in multidivisional corporations that have evolved or organized around product lines. It may also be true of those that have overdone the product segmentation approach, that is, segmented their products so finely that markets and customers have taken a back seat.

> "What must be adopted is a new way of approaching segmentation that drives value, not categorization."

Recent innovations in the supplier-customer relationship may have helped focus on consolidation opportunities. What was formerly viewed as the *bow-tie model* (salespeople selling to purchasing agents) has begun to give way to the *diamond model,* whereby business teams interact with business teams (Figures 4.11 and 4.12). The growing proliferation of (or, at least, publicity *about*) alliances and partnerships—as well as a new understanding of sound business practices in sourcing—have fueled the use of interdisciplinary teams working together to better connect trading partners. Often, this approach is described as *process collaboration* or *comanagement.*

As this profound change occurs in business-to-business relationships, the players begin to identify possible areas of value across the companies, not simply within one product

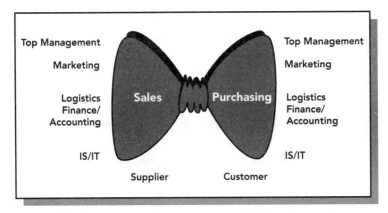

**Figure 4.11** The traditional *bow-tie* selling model.

or transaction. Thus, suppliers often see opportunities in consolidating supply chains across products, across geographies, occasionally across channels, and even across customers and segments. As customers gain more market power, we may even see consolidation across suppliers—such that

**Figure 4.12** The new *diamond* selling model.

product deliveries are the result of multi-orders or multi-replenishments. This is the basic strategy of nonstop logistics in the grocery products industry. Also, it may be manifested in third-party logistics providers, in that they do business with several product suppliers with common customers.

Consolidation strategies can be driven either by cost reduction, the need for reduced capital spending, revenue growth, or both. The intent, again, is to create enhanced value, both for the supplier and the customer. Transforming the management of individual and often independent supply chains into broader, multiproduct chains—consolidated where appropriate from raw material to consumer and back—can yield enormous enterprise-wide value.

## ➤ 4. Identify and Create Common Processes and Systems around the Customer

Supply chains are often distinct entities with global, regional, and local characteristics. Many permutations exist, depending on the diversity of markets, customers, products, and value programs. However, global, regional, and local supply chains are most effective when the business and technology have a great deal of standardization and commonality, and the processes that underlie each of them share characteristics, components, and materials.

Over the years, many companies built processes and systems that differed around the world. Although some of this semicoordinated evolution occurred for a good reason—for example, local regulations, cultural differences, local infrastructure, local technology sophistication, and traditional preferences—most of it occurred because of decentralized decision-making authority and the simple lack of global availability. Recently, however, many companies have learned that the right balance of commonality can mean huge value payoffs in terms of the drivers of market value, that is, growth, cost control, and capital efficiency.

What we want is global, regional, and local supply chains that depend on the market, the product, the customer value proposition, and the common processes. Global supply chains should look the same, as should regional and local chains. Most important, global data should look the same.

This doesn't mean that we can forecast the demand for our product in Malaysia while sitting in Chicago. It does mean, however, that the forecasting *process* for Malaysia, the United States, and Europe should look the same. Demand planners in Chicago should be able to discuss forecasts with demand planners in Southeast Asia using the same terminology, time frame, and methods, and using the same data. Globalization in a profitable manner hinges on common processes and common systems. It is truer in today's environment than ever before.

## ■ SUMMARY

The Chairman of Allied Signal, Larry Bossidy, said, "Despite what you read in the books, it's easier to change culture, attitudes, and people than it is to change process. . . . We have a long way to go in terms of understanding our customers. . . . What worries me most is whether we will be able to satisfy an ever-more-demanding customer."

In this chapter, we examined ways in which companies can do more than *satisfy* an ever-more-demanding customer. Those ways focus on changing the relationship between sales and marketing and key supply chain programs. Effecting push-pull programs that answer market demand in a cost-effective way is one key example. Others include creative segmentation, one-to-one account management, and consumer-direct marketing.

Serving the customer is a continuous process. It means eliminating barriers to buying, crafting targeted value (e.g., bundles), and providing customers with streamlined access to products and services, any time and anywhere in a profitable manner. For example, Becton Dickinson, the medical products company, refers to its "service products": specific value-added services that help customers perform better.

So, if maximizing enterprise value is our strategy, then *delivering customer value profitably* is a key is our mission. And we must redefine our approach to supply chain management to have any hope of succeeding. Unfortunately, there is no cookbook to follow in doing this. The best examples—gleaned from the leaders—are the products of creativity, brainstorming, joint sessions with customers, and executive-driven support of new ideas.

---

## ASK YOUR MANAGERS

1. Do your operations managers collaborate closely with your sales and marketing managers to create customer value?

2. Are you using account management and/or one-to-one marketing concepts to create or evaluate new channels?

3. Have you segmented your markets and your customers to differentiate services accordingly? Can you identify the product/service bundles that you offer to your different channels and customer segments?

4. Does your company maintain up-to-date information on customer satisfaction? How?

5. Do you have customer value strategies? Programs that create win-win value?

6. Do you identify customer value points and then develop consolidation opportunities and systems around specific customers?

7. Can you identify your "service products"? Are they adding value to customer businesses?

# Chapter 5

# Buying Smarter: Strategic Sourcing and Supplier Management

Today, purchased goods and services represent between 50 and 70 percent of a manufacturing company's value potential. Even in service industries, more than half of all services are actually purchased from other organizations. In other words, *the majority* of what a typical company *is* is defined by the components, materials, and services it acquires from outside sources. Conversely, vertical integration is becoming less and less credible, serving only to clutter many organizations with noncore competencies and decrease flexibility in terms of cost structure and adaptability in the marketplace.

With more and more parts, materials, goods, and services purchased outside the organization, companies are also altering the tenor of their supplier relationships. Traditionally, sourcing has been viewed as transactional and functionally competitive: winners cannot exist without losers. This mind-set has long been evident in the behavior of "supply chain bullies" that forcibly extract price reductions or service enhancements from their suppliers without any return in the form of extended contracts, ability to participate in bringing new technologies to market, high schedule visibility, or other investment. Typically, these companies trade short-term gain for long-term pain in the form of reduced innovation, exclusivity, cooperation, and even higher costs. Today, more than ever, suppliers are working to minimize their relationships with such customers.

Leading companies, on the other hand, see that competitive advantage is becoming *less closely tied* to their own innate capabilities: that their success is increasingly defined by the relationships and linkages forged with organizations outside their immediate sphere of influence. They know that today, collaboration—not competition—wins business wars.

In the context of these new supplier/manufacturer paradigms, what are today's most productive sources of competitive advantage? One certain key is to leverage purchasing across the enterprise while capitalizing on common information and information management systems. A second is building strong commodity teams to support supplier partnerships and alliances. A third is to consolidate, using common parts and a reduced supplier set.

Equally critical, however, is developing a fundamental change in perspective: *positioning sourcing as "information brokering and risk management."* In this context, sourcing professionals become managers of external manufacturing or service delivery operations. Their goal is to extend the enterprise across traditional organizational boundaries: to vertically integrate without the capital investment. This virtuality is the essence of strategic sourcing: a change from cost-focused denominator management to corporate revenue and margin contribution. We have found that, on average, enterprise-wide strategic sourcing can reduce the cost of external purchases by 10 to 20 percent. And each dollar saved in a typical purchasing transaction equates (in terms of profit) to a multifold increase in sales. These savings can be compounded by optimizing the physical distribution network, increasing the level of vendor-managed and consigned inventory, and minimizing or eliminating the many causes of weak or inefficient sourcing practices. The most common of these problem practices (and those that are most quickly and easily rectified) include the following:

➤ Several business units independently conduct contract negotiations with the same supplier.

➤ Frequent deviations are made from preferred supplier lists.

➤ Purchasing is done outside negotiated discount contracts.

➤ Insufficient or incomplete advantage is taken of supplier payment terms and conditions.

➤ Purchasing activities are spread through multiple company areas, thus neglecting price (quantity) discounts.

➤ Supplier performance measures are insufficient, misaligned, or do not reflect the true business requirements (more than purchase price).

➤ Suppliers are not certified for quality, delivery performance, capacity, capability, and flexibility.

➤ Company personnel work with too many or too few sources (e.g., for the same product or service).

➤ Inventory visibility is poor throughout the pipeline.

➤ Inappropriate inventory levels are deployed based on demand and sourcing requirements.

➤ The company is unable or unwilling to manage inventory jointly with other supply chain partners.

> *"Sourcing professionals must be recast as managers of external manufacturing or service delivery operations."*

To minimize or alleviate these problems, companies must work to align objectives, interests, values, technologies, and core competencies *across organizational boundaries*. This mission is embodied in the ten altogether doable strategies that comprise the remainder of this chapter.

## ■ 1. CONSIDER SUPPLIERS PART OF YOUR SUPPLY CHAIN: THE EXTENDED SUPPLY CHAIN

Few businesses today will admit to engaging in adversarial relationships with suppliers. Most, in fact, claim to be involved in some form of partnership. Despite all this apparent wisdom, supplier partnering has met with mixed success, particularly across different business sectors. Worse yet, many traditional purchasing managers seem to welcome such setbacks, because they reinforce an old-time, arm's-length preference for bidding and negotiation. In other words, the reality is that many procurement people avoid close relationships with suppliers, because they fear becoming too reliant on partners who might try to exploit the relationship to extract higher prices or force concessions. Obviously, this can be self-defeating. Today's business climate virtually requires that some measure of trust be developed, real relationships be built, and operating information shared, at least with key suppliers. Cooperative pursuit of world-class practices in strategy, systems, processes, and operations is a key element of strategic sourcing (Figure 5.1).

Easy for us to say! After all, sharing information has a pretty ring to it; however, there's still the reality of having live access to your customer's demand and marketing data

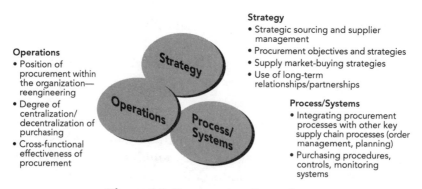

**Operations**
• Position of procurement within the organization—reengineering
• Degree of centralization/decentralization of purchasing
• Cross-functional effectiveness of procurement

**Strategy**
• Strategic sourcing and supplier management
• Procurement objectives and strategies
• Supply market-buying strategies
• Use of long-term relationships/partnerships

**Process/Systems**
• Integrating procurement processes with other key supply chain processes (order management, planning)
• Purchasing procedures, controls, monitoring systems

**Figure 5.1** Key sourcing dimensions.

and to your supplier's cost and planning data. Also, even more frighteningly, they have access to yours! One way to swallow this reality is to understand that high levels of information exchange actually *create* entry barriers. On balance, they make you *less vulnerable,* not more vulnerable. Nevertheless, the key issue is trust: To what degree should a company trust suppliers with valuable operating information? After all, a trusted supplier could become the ally of a competitor, or even *become* a competitor. There is also the question of practical implementation: information sharing is largely predicated on having a reliable, useable technological foundation. But corporate history is riddled with high-cost, low-benefit technology projects, and this one could provide high payback with comparatively low investment.

In general, trust is far more attainable when there is a clear and distinct separation of core competencies between supply chain partners. Naturally, gray areas (core competency overlaps) will enhance feelings of insecurity. This is why many businesses use their core competencies as a strategic means of locking in key customers and suppliers. The relationship between a U.S. disk-drive company (emphasis on design and marketing) and a Japanese manufacturer (strengths in operations and manufacturing) is a good example of an alliance that has led to worldwide preeminence in disk drives. Overall, it is best to start small with a few suppliers and gradually build capabilities, knowledge, and confidence.

---

*"Partnerships work best when there is very little overlap and very little underlap."*

**Scott McNealy**
*Chairman, CEO, and President of Sun Microsystems*

---

Compared with trust, the technology issue is less amorphous. This is because viable means do exist for integrating legacy platforms and architectures (internets and intranets not withstanding). Low-cost integration technology and coordinating mechanisms are great bridges for initiating relationships and building trust among businesses and key supply chain partners. The key is understanding and communicating joint requirements and limitations: a task that typically falls on the sourcing managers of downstream organizations. More often than not, it is their job to ensure the existence of appropriate technology *and* an appropriate strategy for sharing information. Too often, companies lead with technology and fail to recognize the need to develop a shared information strategy.

Point-of-sale data is a good example. Most companies want to have it, yet few are prepared to integrate the data into their decision processes. Although POS data represents a holy grail for many suppliers, a large number of them can do little with it—they don't have the process or the technology to incorporate this data effectively into their operations.

## THE EIGHT COMMANDMENTS OF STRATEGIC SOURCING

1. Business strategy drives sourcing and supplier management.
2. Cross-functional teams manage commodities throughout the sourcing life cycle.
3. Unique commodity and supplier characteristics dictate appropriate sourcing and supplier-management strategies.
4. Companies must leverage enterprise-wide sourcing to achieve maximum benefits.
5. Benefits are not sustainable without institutionalizing process and infrastructure changes.
6. Leadership plays a vital role in driving change.
7. Joint work with suppliers (design to delivery) is better than trying it alone.
8. Capitalize on existing initiatives and leverage scarce resources—focus on key commodities.

Personal relationships are another area that may be over-looked by companies seeking to build a supplier-inclusive supply chain. However, the power of these relationships—particularly at the senior level—outweighs even the significance of technical or alignment issues. Some businesses have recognized and formalized this key source of competitive advantage by creating top-to-top programs in which key decision makers meet on a regular basis. Supplier councils (whose purpose is to address the views of key suppliers) are a successful variation on this theme. It is also critical that executive managers meet regularly with the key decision makers of each supply chain partner.

# ■ 2. ORGANIZE EFFECTIVELY AND GET THE RIGHT PEOPLE

Many businesses claim to have built customer-facing organizations. However, although some have actually established multiple customer links across the organization (as opposed to relying on traditional sales-to-purchase pressure points), most attempts fail to meet expectations. One reason is uneven allocation of power and the resultant failure of internal functions to align themselves productively. In fast-moving, consumer goods firms, for example, brand management and sales may lead. In an engineering-driven firm, design may dominate. In the retail environment, the buying or merchandising group may be preeminent. However, supply chain integration requires balanced, multidisciplinary action. Downstream operations (internal or external) seldom care whether the business is brand led. What they want is competitively priced goods delivered on time, as promised, and with good quality.

Thus, top-performing sourcing organizations understand internal and downstream approaches and align them with those of key suppliers. They manage the gap between goals and perceptions of buyers and sellers in the supply chain, and suboptimize narrow goals in one or more areas to reach broader business objectives.

In a recent study on partnerships and alliances,[1] a key finding was that supply chain weakness often stems from a misalignment of perceptions, goals, and objectives *within companies.* To overcome these problems, companies must align operations, marketing, and sourcing in terms of goals, targets, and processes; then they must integrate relationships with key customers and suppliers.

Companies must *organize effectively:* make sourcing part of the fabric of their organizations—a mission-critical component. Figure 5.2 depicts a framework for an organization-wide system of sourcing and supplier management that stresses concurrency by

➤ Defining *and* implementing objectives

➤ Pursuing operational effectiveness *and* executional efficiency

➤ Simultaneously addressing cost, innovation, *and* supply issues (no trade-offs)

This framework highlights several characteristics of a cutting-edge sourcing organization:

1. Develop clear and aligned objectives and targets by commodity.

2. Ensure accountability for sourcing *and* for the organization.

3. Develop a solid infrastructure of information, information systems, reporting relationships, and performance management.

4. Implement commodity life cycle and generational planning using a multidisciplinary commodity team that receives executive management visibility.

**Figure 5.2** Building a coordinated supplier/sourcing management capability.

Then comes the big question: To centralize or not to centralize? Often swayed by outside influences, many organizations vacillate between a decentralized structure (when staff are placed in autonomous business units to select and evaluate suppliers, and to negotiate and execute contracts, prices, terms, and conditions) and a centralized structure (in which these activities are consolidated at the organization level). The pendulum swings every few years.

Many companies seem to have more concerns about centralizing operations than they do about making them effective. Most of those worries focus on issues of responsiveness and empowerment: a perceived loss of the ability to ensure consistent supply levels and make informed choices about suppliers. Many managers also believe that better prices are the exclusive motivator for a system of centralized buying. This may be true in some cases, but it does not mean that this is the sole rationalization for centralized approaches.

Instead, problems with centralized buying are often the result of inappropriate metrics. One example is basing purchase prices solely on negotiated, *compared-to-last-year* increases or *purchased part variances*. This approach optimizes the initial purchase price reduction function at the expense of the life-cycle process.

Current business trends lean toward more decentralization. The reasoning is that an increasingly demand-driven and consumer-centric marketplace may be better served by people and departments with more autonomy. Accordingly, greater potential for responsiveness exists in a decentralized environment. The issue, though, may be a loss of standardization and a concomitant set of missed opportunities; that is, less buying clout and a diminished ability to develop sustainable, mutually beneficial relationships with key suppliers. Negotiating on a long-term basis, wholly decentralized buying organizations are at a disadvantage; often, however, that gap can be successfully filled by information. Like so many business processes, *sourcing operations are only as good as the information they share.* In fact, companies with sophisticated information-sharing mechanisms can deploy what is probably the most common-sense solution: a hybrid (centralized/decentralized) sourcing business in which responsive-

---

### OPERATIONAL INNOVATION: REDUCING THE NUMBER OF SUPPLIERS

**A major financial services firm** realized that 48 percent of its 55,000 purchase orders were for amounts under $500. According to the CEO, "With 36,000 vendors to manage, we spent nearly half our time counting nickels and dimes." After addressing the issues, they reduced their supply base to 17,000 and issued only 3,000 purchase orders in 1996, raising the quality of inputs and reducing the cost of goods in the process.

ness, flexibility, buying power, and relationship development and management are all attainable. Figure 5.3 outlines one such successful hybrid.

> *"The centralization/decentralization hybrid is a paradigm for the global marketplace."*

The reality, however, is that supplier management approaches emphasizing *total systems cost* (or total acquisition cost) offer the greatest benefits to the overall enterprise—regardless of whether the purchasing environment is centralized or decentralized. Nevertheless, the centralization/decentralization hybrid is, in our opinion, a paradigm for the global marketplace. After all, globalization means deploying global resources *effectively,* not centrally. In the hybrid model, characteristics of a centralized approach favor the need to negotiate and leverage relationships worldwide. Conversely, successful penetration of the global marketplace requires strong segmentation and mass customization skills, which favor a decentralized approach. The net effect is more purchasers with better management controls. There are several examples of large (and sometimes, global) companies that have experienced success with such hybrid-sourcing

| Activities Managed Centrally | Activities Managed Locally |
|---|---|
| ➤ Contract negotiations | ➤ Order release |
| ➤ Supplier selection for key enterprise commodities | ➤ Order receipt |
| ➤ Supplier performance relationships | ➤ On-site expediting |
| ➤ Liaison with corporate management | ➤ Liaison to central sourcing |
| ➤ Training and development | ➤ Supplier management for local-use material |

**Figure 5.3** A centralization/decentralization hybrid.

models in a wide variety of industries, from high technology/electronics to consumer packaged goods, and from automobiles to retail.

Last, but not least, get the right people. Obtaining and developing human capital is among the biggest supplier-management challenges that companies face. A brief list of the twenty-first-century sourcing and supply manager's most desirable traits includes:

➤ A "T"-skills profile (a clear area of specialization combined with a broader understanding of how various business functions interrelate)

➤ A global perspective

➤ Strong relationship-building skills (people must deal with complex hierarchical and networked relationships, because many suppliers are simultaneously suppliers, competitors, and customers)

➤ A strong understanding of the company's business model (how, precisely, the company makes money and where the costs, drivers, and impacts lie)

➤ A strong understanding of the industry and its dynamics

Unfortunately, too many procurement professionals have become steeped in transaction-type buying. Unlike marketing people, who (theoretically) are trained to build and maintain long-term customer relationships, many buyers have always been judged on metrics that are not conducive to effecting cooperative relationships. In the final analysis, you reward what you measure and you get what you reward. Thus, the right people must be accompanied by new sourcing and supplier-management metrics that are geared to the business model and that drive collaborative behavior when necessary, and ferociously cost-cutting behavior when that is necessary.

# ■ 3. DEVELOP COMMODITY TEAMS

Highly effective buying organizations often deploy commodity teams. Sometimes known as sourcing families, commodity teams focus expertise and resources on high-dollar, strategically important products and services. They also seek to reconcile competing functional perspectives and resource use. Lastly, commodity teams emphasize a total-life-cycle and cost perspective, as well as strategic, proactive supplier management. *They are responsible for the commodity, its costs, and its inventory levels, through its (multigenerational) life cycle, as well as programs dealing with supplier ownership of material, supplier development, and supplier management of the material.*

> "Sourcing operations are only as good as
> the information they share."

Most often, commodity teams are structured around products or services that have similar technical characteristics or applications, and that are usually acquired from a common supply base in which aggregated buying will increase relative leverage or yield other mutual benefits. These teams can address from 85 to 95 percent of an organization's annual spending in direct materials, indirect materials, and services.

Commodity teams rely on the organization's business strategy and underlying guiding principles to develop sourcing strategies, implement changes, and monitor performance on an ongoing basis. Figure 5.4 provides the basic steps for implementing such a construct. For most organizations, we believe the commodity-team approach is a fundamentally better way to manage the enterprise-wide buying process.

Lastly, whereas several leading companies across a wide number of industries have successfully adopted the com-

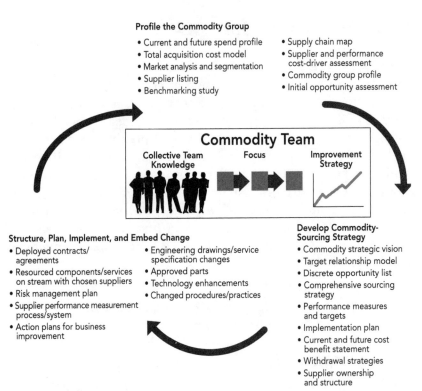

**Profile the Commodity Group**

- Current and future spend profile
- Total acquisition cost model
- Market analysis and segmentation
- Supplier listing
- Benchmarking study
- Supply chain map
- Supplier and performance cost-driver assessment
- Commodity group profile
- Initial opportunity assessment

**Commodity Team**

Collective Team Knowledge  Focus  Improvement Strategy

**Structure, Plan, Implement, and Embed Change**

- Deployed contracts/agreements
- Resourced components/services on stream with chosen suppliers
- Risk management plan
- Supplier performance measurement process/system
- Action plans for business improvement
- Engineering drawings/service specification changes
- Approved parts
- Technology enhancements
- Changed procedures/practices

**Develop Commodity-Sourcing Strategy**

- Commodity strategic vision
- Target relationship model
- Discrete opportunity list
- Comprehensive sourcing strategy
- Performance measures and targets
- Implementation plan
- Current and future cost benefit statement
- Withdrawal strategies
- Supplier ownership and structure

**Figure 5.4** Commodity teams develop sourcing strategies, implement changes, and monitor performance on an ongoing basis.

modity-team approach to sourcing, other approaches to teaming also produce positive, enterprise-wide benefits, and are often used in conjunction with commodity teams:

➤ *Key supplier account representatives* are staff dedicated to relationship management. Sometimes deployed as a response to a corporate winnowing of suppliers, they work to build supplier relationships, review business processes, make technology projections, manage supplier-council or supplier-panel discussions, identify joint critical success factors, and review expectations. Key supplier account representatives spend from 80 to 90 percent of their time with suppliers or internal customers.

➤ *Supplier councils* (generally consisting of about 10 to 20 key suppliers) may be implemented to provide feedback and dialogue. Supply council members discuss business plans, new supply management initiatives, and proposed changes to company policies. In effect, they are a sourcing-steering group.

## ■ 4. PRACTICE GLOBAL SOURCING AND SUPPLIER MANAGEMENT

Unlike traditional, transactional purchasing or procurement, strategic sourcing encompasses supply-related activities throughout the product or service life cycle: from initial concept through disposal and across technology generations. Thinking and acting globally is a logical extension of this concept. Granted, most companies today do procure globally. That is, they buy product internationally to supply their facilities and customers internationally. However, international procurement is not the same as global sourcing. Global sourcing looks at the best source of product to supply global operations. It makes product life-cycle decisions based on purchase price, lead-time delivery, technology, flexibility in response to schedule changes, and economic and political stability.

> *"International procurement is not the same*
> *as global sourcing."*

Managing upstream relationships globally requires an increasingly complex array of networks and alliances. The potential to add significant value is vast, which is why more and more companies position strategic sourcing as a core competency. However, because sourcing is a suboptimized, largely unilateral process in many companies, global sourcing often devolves to regional purchasing, with components or materials purchased in sequential, open-market transactions that are sometimes adversarial and occasionally political.

Not surprisingly, working with international suppliers is tricky, if for no other reason than the increased distances involved. Thus, a key consideration is whether to work with foreign suppliers directly or to use intermediaries. The indirect approach usually has less risk (but higher costs) and, thus, is more useful to companies that are new to international procurement. Typically, indirect international sourcing involves import merchants, commission houses (to handle consignments for foreign governments), and trading firms (import and export). For each, purchasing is essentially a domestic transaction. Organizations may also consider the use of an import broker that, for a fee, helps locate suppliers in foreign countries.

Because of the complexity of global sourcing issues, many organizations use international purchasing organizations (IPOs). In addition to identifying and selecting sources, IPOs often negotiate with suppliers and, assuming agreements are reached, prepare contracts. Advantages include:

## OPERATIONAL INNOVATION: ELECTRONIC COMMERCE IN PROCUREMENT

**General Electric** recently developed a "Trading Process Network": a secure Web site that connects GE to its suppliers. As a result, the company's GE Lighting unit in Cleveland has cut procurement time in half and reduced raw materials purchasing costs by 10 to 15 percent.*

*Tom Stein, "Orders from Chaos," *Information Week,* no. 636 (23 June 1997): 44–6, 50 ff.

➤ Better supplier relationships (facilitated by face-to-face cooperation)

➤ Lower procurement costs (no middlemen)

➤ Enhanced buying opportunities

➤ Improved quality control (on-site inspection and communication)

➤ Positive negotiating results (based on locally obtained information)

➤ Facilitated trade operations

Working directly, the principal global sourcing issue is coordination. Recent advances in electronic communication help, but they are by no means the solution. In broad terms, parties must determine contract provisions, including legal recourse, quality control, conditions for order changes, cancellation clauses and inspection, and taxes. More broadly, direct global sourcing also warrants consideration of:

➤ Applicable federal and foreign regulations

➤ Evaluation

➤ Specification/pricing

➤ Financing

➤ Negotiation

➤ Traffic

➤ Customs issues

➤ Tariffs, quotas, licensing, and patent and trademark laws

Reaping the benefits of global sourcing is a long-term prospect that requires a significant amount of organizational resources to sustain. In an international context, understanding and respect are important, but enhanced knowledge of international practices and customs is critical. One advantage of global sourcing is the forced development of an array of offshore relationships that might not have been discovered otherwise. In the final analysis, however, *landed costs* (i.e., total cost) and access to high-quality materials and technology are the reasons to consider international procurement and procurement structures.

## ■ 5. FOCUS ON TOTAL COSTS

*Total systems-based costing* underlies the entire premise of delivering value through sourcing. Initial purchase price may always be a starting point, but it is paramount that companies move sourcing from its traditional reliance on reducing purchase-price cost and toward minimizing total systems cost (or total acquisition costs) and enhancing supply capability and flexibility.

Looking beyond initial purchase price to total acquisition cost is a good way to begin. Quality, price, delivery, and service all have a stake in value gained or lost. *Each is a contributor to an overall acquisition cost.* Other costs that are not so obvious are the costs to possess the materials, application and inspection costs, and internal and external failure costs. Figure 5.5 identifies some of the key cost buckets assigned to these broad

---

### OPERATION INNOVATION: LEVERAGING SUPPLIER SKILLS

Engineers sometimes design a part or a product without considering whether an existing supplier could do the same thing in a more cost-effective and timely manner. For several years, **AT&T** has involved buyers in new product development through its "cost-effective product introduction buyer program." Engineers and preferred suppliers work together to develop new products. The result is low-cost reuse of standard parts and a decrease in product development time.*

*James Carbone, "A Buyer's Place Is in the Design Lab," *Purchasing*, 120, no. 3 (7 March 1996): 59.

| Major Cost Area | Cost Elements |
|---|---|
| Acquisition costs | ➤ Labor to process purchase orders<br>➤ Computer(s) to prepare, track, and verify orders and shipments<br>➤ Labor to expedite late deliveries<br>➤ Building and office space<br>➤ Supervision of sourcing process<br>➤ Labor to prepare and process multiple bids on low-value items |
| Possession costs | ➤ Operating and depreciating inventory-holding space<br>➤ Heat and other utilities<br>➤ Janitorial and guard personnel<br>➤ Routine and special building maintenance and repair<br>➤ Taxes on land, building, and inventory<br>➤ Insurance on building and equipment<br>➤ Liability insurance<br>➤ Yearly interest on loans made to purchase MRO items<br>➤ Estimated loss of return on inventory capital<br>➤ Average yearly loss from materials obsolescence and pilferage<br>➤ In-plant damage or deterioration<br>➤ Labor to receive, stock, identify, move, and maintain materials<br>➤ Extra accounting hours necessitated for inventory control<br>➤ Supervisory cost of inventory<br>➤ Top management time spent solving inventory problems |
| Application costs | ➤ Labor to engineer and specify products for new applications<br>➤ Labor to upgrade products for a more efficient operation<br>➤ Downtime due to wrong products<br>➤ Training personnel to use products |

**Figure 5.5** Total costing: some nonobvious cost categories.

| Major Cost Area | Cost Elements |
| --- | --- |
| Inspection costs | ➤ Labor to investigate and conduct inspection<br>➤ Material and storage costs associated with inspections<br>➤ Special equipment and/or procedures for inspections |
| Internal/ external failure costs | ➤ Line pulls and associates failures<br>➤ Warranty costs<br>➤ Reuse/scrap costs<br>➤ Impositions on bottleneck operations |

**Figure 5.5** *(Continued)*

categories. Figure 5.6 depicts a generic *total acquisition cost model* and some of the general categories of cost drivers. Identifying total acquisition costs involves quantifying all the relevant cost elements (some companies assess their impact by assigning category weights and future needs) and setting targets for future performance. Some companies use activity-based costing to arrive at these costs and zero-based budgeting

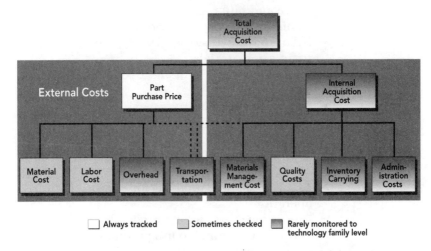

**Figure 5.6** Developing a total acquisition cost model requires an understanding of key cost drivers.

to set targets (although it is often more difficult). Others (and they fare equally well or better) set targets based on industry and competitive standards, or "stretch goals."

The next challenge is knowing where the money is spent. Few organizations know exactly what they buy, and even fewer use this information to drive strategic and tactical decisions about future sourcing endeavors. Nevertheless, understanding this is essential. Developing a snapshot of the total procurement spend is arduous, and it is usually complicated by the variety of systems deployed by most organizations.

The key is to focus first on high-dollar items. Decision support tools can help. These systems consider various sourcing parameters; calculate supplier ratings; assess supplier dependencies; and evaluate opportunities for supplier reductions, national buying agreements, and cross-commodity leverage. Such tools may also help automate the scoring and monitoring of supplier performance and risk using customized, objective, rules-based scoring models.

The next step is to determine where and how money is spent with outside providers of materials and services: a process sometimes called *spend characterization*. Using software tools to facilitate data collection and analysis, this activity characterizes the organizational spend along categories of product-buy classes to include commodity analysis, supplier's industry analysis, supplier's process costs, leading practices and benchmarks, and margin analysis. The primary driver in assessing suppliers and procurement spending is a fact-based, hard-cost analysis. Such analyses can help decisions in supplier consolidation, volume purchase negotiations, and other expense-reduction activities.

## ■ 6. SIMPLIFY

Processes that are simpler work better. In the case of sourcing, this means minimizing the need for deals and complex pricing, and focusing instead on quality and net delivered cost. For example, spend less time developing rebates and claw backs, and use that time to understand and improve the underlying fundamentals of the relationship and their contribution to the value perceived by customers and consumers. One strategy is to make *formula-based* pricing decisions by relying on industry and government indices.

However, a key in sourcing-process simplification is to *work more closely with fewer suppliers.* Strong relationships with a (manageable) stable of high-quality suppliers afford companies more leverage in the marketplace. They also position the business to respond more quickly to market shifts and demands. Also, when less efficient or less desirable suppliers are weeded out, the overall supplier/customer supply chain becomes stronger. Supplier reduction, when coupled with increased parts standardization (increased commonality), also cuts the number of transactions associated with purchasing. This rationalization—particularly when attaching the associated costs of many noncritical procured material classes—is an excellent way to reduce total acquisition costs.

| Successful Supplier Reductions | |
|---|---|
| Company | Change ( % ) |
| Xerox | −90 |
| Centerior Energy | −90 |
| Motorola | −70 |
| Digital Equipment | −67 |
| Westinghouse | −45 |
| General Motors | −45 |
| Ford | −44 |
| Texas Instruments | −36 |
| Dun & Bradstreet | −53 |
| Allied Signal Aerospace | −20 |

Not surprisingly, far closer linkages must exist between a company and the key suppliers it chooses to retain. Ideally, there will be a state of *concurrent procurement,* in which early supplier involvement helps to reduce design, manufacturing, or service delivery cycle times. Key suppliers may even join the design, manufacturing, or service operations process. In this scenario, sourcing professionals manage (or even lead) upstream manufacturing or service delivery operations. Other mechanisms for working more effectively with a smaller stable of suppliers include supplier conferences and councils, flexible contracting, strategic benchmarking (or information sharing), key supplier account management, and integrated information flows.

---

*"The key to sourcing-process simplification is to work more closely with fewer suppliers."*

---

Importantly, fewer suppliers does not necessarily mean more vertical integration. Working more closely with fewer suppliers is, more accurately, virtual manufacturing or *vertical integration without the capital investment.* Outsourcing is a perfect example: companies acquire products or services in a partnership environment that lacks the burden of heavy capital expenditures or equity exchanges and help ensure operational and cost flexibility.

## ■ 7. LET SUPPLIERS MANAGE IT

Strategic supplier management means finding innovative ways to unleash supplier creativity and take advantage of supplier expertise. Here are three examples.

### ➤ Vendor-Managed Inventories

Vendor-managed inventories (VMI) make sense in the same way that maintaining stores of finished products can benefit the manufacturer's customers. These inventory management partnerships inspire joint decisions about inventory levels, replenishment, and locations—each of which is predicated on shared supply chain goals, short- and long-term incentives, and real-time information. For the buyer, reduced inventory-carrying costs and improved service levels often result, which, in turn, create the opportunity for suppliers to improve their demand/supply and inventory management efforts. Greater collaboration also results in better monitoring of material usage, demand, availability, and service levels through information transfer and sharing. And, as many companies have discovered, reductions in systemwide safety stock are typically associated with vendor-managed inventories. Such VMI programs take many forms: suppliers managing floor stock on the manufacturing floor, maintaining plant-adjacent warehouses and stocks for quick turnaround and flexibility, delivery as needed (or scheduled in small time increments) directly to the manufacturing or configuration line, and, in some instances, accepting orders and fulfilling directly to the store or customer. A further variant is comanaged inventory, in which the supplier and the customer manage inventory jointly.

## OPERATIONAL INNOVATION: STRENGTHENING SUPPLIER RELATIONSHIPS

**Ford Motor Co.** has identified approximately 15 minority suppliers with good track records (long-term/preferred component or service providers). Ford pays a portion of those suppliers' interest payments on new commercial loans that support growth coming from Ford business. Ford is also considering providing technical assistance on a case-by-case basis.*

*Kevin R. Fitzgerald, "Automakers' Strategies Must Change at the First Tier," *Purchasing*, 121, no. 9 (12 December 1996): 65(2).

*"The great advantages of consortium buying are minimization of transaction costs and the sharing of operating insights and best practices."*

Obviously, well-managed vendor-managed inventory programs require high levels of collaboration. Centralized visibility and control are key, along with fluency in demand management, inventory deployment, and continuous replenishment. Companies seeking increased vendor responsibility for managing inventories need to pursue complementary objectives, skills, and capabilities. Equally important is the senior-level commitment of financial resources, information technology, and operational systems. In return, suppliers get long-term capacity forecasts (to stabilize their own operations and capital expenditures, reduce planning and selling costs, and grow with the buyer in terms of technology, innovation, scale, and volume).

## ➤ Consortium (Multicompany Group) Buying

This is another opportunity that requires extensive coordination between buyers and suppliers; it also requires good forward planning capabilities. As is the case with VMI, a great deal of management oversight and initiative is needed to implement consortium-buying programs. Their great advantages, however, are minimization of transaction costs and the sharing of operating insights and best practices. Moreover, inferior and low-performing suppliers are quickly identified and marginalized as consortium members share their experiences. Oftentimes, consortium groups will seek third-party suppliers to manage certain buying arrangements. FedEx, for example, is one of the country's best known and most successful practitioners of consortium buying.

## ➤ Outsourcing

Outsourcing is now practiced by 85 percent of North American and European multinational companies, and, according to a recent *Economist* poll, many companies expect to increase their outsourcing levels over the next three years. Outsourcing differs from subcontracting in that the outsourcing organization divests itself of the assets, infrastructure, people, and competencies that it previously used to do the work. Freeing these (often constrained) resources allows the company to concentrate on tasks and activities that deliver clear, competitive advantage and higher returns. In the procurement area, many companies choose to outsource their purchasing and purchasing-planning functions to third parties. As these providers grow in scope, scale, and expertise, this trend promises to grow.

Companies must be able to understand and articulate the business drivers (including complexity of components, supplier base and operations, material costs, and technology trends) that are telling them to outsource their sourcing activities. They must also work to prepare their own organi-

---

### OUTSOURCING IN THE AUTO INDUSTRY

An important outsourcing trend in the auto industry is the use of tiered suppliers to provide complete systems such as a door module or a dashboard/cockpit module. With this approach, one first-tier supplier is required to take full responsibility for coordinating and managing second- and third-tier suppliers and for assembling and delivering the completed module. For the supplier (particularly those on the first tier), this approach can increase productivity and improve economies of scale. For the manufacturer, benefits include faster response for new product development, focused competencies, reduced inventories, and simplified transactions.

zation for its new relationship with an outsourced operation, as the skill sets needed to manage "outsourced sourcing" are different from traditional purchasing in terms of management involvement, material, cost and scope control, and a broader understanding of the business model.

Volkswagen, for example, has innovated even further in outsourcing supplier-management activities. Recently, VW opened its newest truck plant in Brazil, based on a concept called modular consortia. Roberto Baretti, VW's director of operations at the plant, describes the operation by saying that, "VW provides the house and the suppliers the furniture."

## ■ 8. LEVERAGE INFORMATION TECHNOLOGY AND ELECTRONIC COMMERCE

Fueled by powerful trends, the growth in information technology services and applications is enormous, and promises to continue at an even more accelerated pace. The impact on sourcing and supplier management will be profound. After all, information technology is a key driver of the new sourcing model. And sourcing processes are among the main beneficiaries of integrated information capture, that is, information captured at a single point in the supply chain and then shared in multiple contexts and points of use. The following trends are worth monitoring and exploiting:

➤ The drive to reach "Year 2000" compliance (resulting in wholesale replacement of current systems)

➤ Development in client/server and distributed systems technologies

➤ Developments in three seemingly adversarial, but really complementary, sets of technologies: "thin clients," powerful desktop machines, and new generations of mainframe computers

➤ Advances in technologies such as smart cards

➤ Advances in data management, storage, and mining technologies

➤ The explosive growth in the Internet and Web-based technologies and the resultant rise in electronic commerce

➤ Increasingly sophisticated demand/supply-planning and -scheduling systems

➤ Developments in tracking, distribution, and monitoring technologies

These technologies can easily provide significant competitive advantages and must be used as the basis for operational innovation.

Integrated information capture requires a unified effort by supply chain partners to identify relevant data and establish the information capabilities needed to make sharing happen. One major car manufacturer, for example, exchanges no advance shipping notices, invoices, or check requests with its exclusive radiator supplier. When a truck rolls off the assembly line, the company knows the vehicle has a radiator and, thus, authorizes payment. The same opportunities apply to service industries: the cost of processing a conventional airline ticket is estimated at eight times that of processing an e-ticket.

> *"Information technology is a key driver*
> *of the new sourcing model."*

Enterprise resource-planning (ERP) systems currently dominate the landscape as companies strive to integrate and standardize enterprise-wide and interenterprise business information systems. Addressing the normal transactions associated with supply-base interactions, these systems typically offer materials management or procurement modules that purport to optimize all purchasing processes with work-flow-driven processing functions. Many also have the ability

> **OPERATIONAL INNOVATION:**
> **GLOBAL SOURCING**
>
> **DuPont's** global business units have formed a corporate sourc-
> ing group. Each unit has its own sourcing leader who works
> closely with the corporate sourcing professionals. The corpo-
> rate sourcing group focuses on efficiency in sourcing and pur-
> chasing. This maximizes corporate purchasing leverage and
> cost control.*
>
> *Andrew Wood, "Purchasing's Power: Strengthening the Supply Chain,"
> *Chemical Week*, 158, no. 29 (31 July 1996): 25–7.

to assist with tactical issues, supplier evaluation, procurement
and warehousing cost analysis, and integrated invoice verifi-
cation. But beware: it is highly likely that a company will have
to augment these with other systems that focus on and spe-
cialize in key operational areas. It's the classic operational-
information systems department trade-off between good
functionality and systems standardization.

A critical component of any suite of systems should be
early warning systems that can obtain and summarize operational data into executive information: in effect, providing
an "operational dashboard." Such systems, when effectively
used, can link internal and external business processes
involving customers and suppliers to form overlapping supply chains from procurement through sales.

The rapid growth of electronic commerce has changed the
dynamics of procurement and will continue to do so, with
growth in electronic commerce projected to be in the hundreds of billions of dollars within five years. Electronic commerce can be defined as the buying and selling of goods and
services electronically and has obviously been fueled by the
Internet and the development of Web-based technologies—
truly replacing inventory with information.

It is important to note that a technology-enabled, paperless environment does not immediately imply a business

partnership. Multifaceted relationships among companies are not a prerequisite to the effective sharing of information. In fact, the hybrid (centralized/decentralized) sourcing model emphasizes *differing levels of relationships* based on varying business contexts and product-buy classes. And most of these (particularly products that can be represented digitally, with many potential suppliers, and that can be easily compared with each other) are likely to be arm's-length and transactional.

Nevertheless, two fundamental behaviors *are* essential to the productive, electronic exchange of information: *coordination* (leveraging IT to synchronize the flows of information, intelligence, and cash through the supply chain) and *cooperation* (willingness to share enough information and resources to make coordination happen). These perspectives must ride on top of an overall sourcing technology strategy that encompasses six basic areas:

1. Tactical planning software and decision support tools
2. Core transaction processing and purchase execution software
3. EDI technologies and Web-based technologies
4. Imaging, forms automation, and product identification technologies (e.g., bar coding)
5. Automated purchase order/invoice processing and payment, up to invoiceless processing and two-way matching
6. Integration with suppliers' and providers' information systems (particularly ordering, scheduling, and inventory management)

Beyond EDI, open systems technology is beginning to offer features and functionality that dramatically reduce the time needed to accurately and quickly identify, select, approve, and order goods. For example, electronic multivendor catalogs; automated order creation; and reconciliation,

---

**OPERATIONAL INNOVATION: REDUCING NUMBER OF SUPPLIERS**

**Boeing** and **Airbus** are partnering with select suppliers to further improve cost efficiency and better manage their supply chains. In the aerospace industry, these initiatives are particularly critical, because 60 to 80 percent of an airplane is purchased from outside the company. In so doing, both companies have reduced the number of first-tier suppliers.*

*John Crampton, "Lean Manufacturing Is Just a Start," *Interavia Business & Technology*, 51, no. 602 (August 1996): 24–5.

---

tracking, and reporting capabilities have been shown to reduce the time to requisition, approve, and process orders by 50 percent for certain categories of purchased items.

## ➤ Justifying Electronic Procurement

Electronic sourcing and supplier management holds great promise for companies and enterprises willing to leverage technology to streamline processes and reduce costs. However, like all types of information technology, demonstrating a clear return on investment can be difficult. In electronic procurement, three areas typically house the most quantifiable benefits and the most compelling ROI: improved productivity, improved inventory management, and better overall supply chain management.

### *Improved Productivity*

Traditional requisitioning and procurement processes undermine productivity in many ways. To begin with, most activities are dragged out by time-consuming handoffs, travel, and waiting periods. Electronic procurement improves productivity by:

➤ Reducing the time spent searching for quotes and product selection, order status and availability, correcting errors, and processing invoices and payments

➤ Reducing reviews, checking requisitions, and limiting the involvement of requisitioners and clerks

➤ Improving field-buyer productivity through focus on a reduced supplier set and on-line interchange of information with these suppliers

➤ Reducing manual purchase order processing and error rates (and the resultant rework)

### *Improved Inventory Management*

Enhanced inventory management (achieved without risk to customers or operations) is an important result of electronic

---

**OPERATIONAL INNOVATION:
HYBRID CENTRALIZATION/
DECENTRALIZATION OF PURCHASING**

Purchasing at **Hoechst Celanese**'s Fiber and Films Division is decentralized. However, a centralized main purchasing function has been developed that breaks up procurement into sourcing categories. A category leader is assigned to each of the sourcing categories and acts as a product manager. Hoechst Celanese has also consolidated its supplier base from about 4,000 companies down to 20. Cost savings and improved sourcing are the main benefits of this strategy.*

*Alice Naude, "Source Reengineering: Focusing on Efficiency in Sourcing and Procurement Is the Newest Industry Strategy to Control Costs," *Chemical Marketing Reporter*, 250, no. 3 (15 July 1996): SR8(2).

procurement investment. For example, using a Web-based system that carries real-time and near-real-time information about supplier inventories and product availability, results in a better, broader, and more timely view into the warehouse and improved tracking and analysis of procurement needs. Additional benefits include:

➤ Lower material handling costs through fewer material moves on the road and in the warehouse, and the consequent reduction in documentation costs

➤ Reduced inventory levels and carrying costs, including the all-important excess and obsolete write-off costs

➤ Improved ability to analyze purchasing patterns and evaluate supplier performance

➤ Opportunity to improve service levels by decreasing cycle times from order to delivery, and increasing the ability to make and communicate changes in order and supply position

### *Positioning the Extended Enterprise for Improved Supply Chain Management*

The advantages of electronic commerce permeate the complete supply chain in the forms of lower costs (including working capital and supply chain assets); greater organizational and transactional simplicity (e.g., dealing with fewer suppliers); reduced time-to-market and delivery times, and more expedient, collaborative problem solving. But even greater and more strategic benefits lie on the horizon, as corporate supply chains move toward the extended supply chain. Tomorrow's integrated (virtual) enterprise will compete as a single, extended supply chain, with a linked infrastructure, integrated processes, and collaboration.

## ■ 9. TO ENHANCE SOURCING AUTOMATION, TRY PROCUREMENT CARDS

Procurement cards are a simple way to reduce costs, facilitate point-of-use buying, and minimize the inherent conflicts that arise when buyers and users differ. Consider that a typical purchase order can cost between $100 and $120 per transaction. Much of this expense can be avoided with a supplier credit system that specifies certain SKUs and dollar limits. In other words, procurement cards are a sort of charge account in which balances accrue until a time or dollar limit is reached and an invoice is cut. Studies have shown that procurement card usage drastically cuts the time and cost of processing invoices and making payments. A whole host of companies use procurement cards, and their number is growing as companies discover their benefits. Among these are massive (35 to 90 percent) reductions in purchase processing time and costs, improved procurement management (for example, less paperwork and improved controls, better and customized reporting, improved cost allocation and, importantly, total alignment with current procurement priorities and approved sources) and, ultimately, easier use and reduced cycle times for the user of the parts. And this applies to supplier *and* customer.

## ■ 10. PARTNER SMART

The first premise of supplier relationships is consistency. Predictable supplier relationships and transactions result in lower total acquisition costs.

---

*"As interactions with suppliers become more predictable, Bell South's acquisition costs will be lowered."*

**Jack Wagner**
*Manager of Procurement Strategy,*
*Research and Analysis, Bell South*

---

```
┌─────────────────────────────────────────────────────────┐
│          ┌──────────────────────────────┐               │
│          │   OPERATIONAL INNOVATION:    │               │
│          │     COMMODITY TEAMS          │               │
│          └──────────────────────────────┘               │
```

**Motorola** uses commodity teams to achieve annual performance goals such as "68 percent quality improvement" and
"tenfold cycle time improvement." The teams include buyers,
design engineers, quality people, and sometimes manufacturing and finance. Each team is dedicated to a particular commodity such as plastics, capacitors, and semiconductors, and
each team is responsible for managing the supply base. Additionally, the commodity teams are responsible for ensuring
that identical processes and metrics are applied consistently
by the suppliers.*

*Tim Minahan, "Purchasing Rebuilds to Battle Poor Quality," *Purchasing*,
122, no. 1 (16 January 1997): 53(3).

What characterizes smart partnerships? For one thing, an
approach that emphasizes mutual value and total system
cost. Another is, via formal and informal processes, regularly sharing information on plans, customer needs, capacity utilization, and supply chain costs. Two basic beliefs
guide this approach: "Information can replace inventory,"
and "Risks are shared along with rewards." This sort of relationship does not come intuitively to many companies.
Regardless of the nature of the relationship, buyers and sellers react to one another based on learned behaviors. Thus, it
is important to 1) select supply chain partners on the basis
of mutual interest and values, 2) understand fully the core
competencies of these businesses, and 3) be clear about the
power balance in each relationship.

> *"The bottom line is that partnering should be
> powered first by enlightened self-interest."*

By and large, the most successful partnerships have built-
in market mechanisms. For example, a major aircraft com-

pany will occasionally compete elements of its sourcing business just to gauge what the market is doing, but it does not require suppliers to share their internal costs. However, it does expect its procurement managers to know more about what the materials *should* cost (by relying on such techniques as parametric cost estimating) than the suppliers themselves do—an excellent practice to emulate.

Smart sourcing partnerships also acknowledge that not all supply chain partners are equal. Their focus is on developing a portfolio of partnering strategies. Moving to collaborative relationships with all suppliers defeats the point: true partnerships are too resource-intensive to be widely practical. Furthermore, sensitive company information should not be shared with a wide variety of outsiders. Selectivity is critical. The bottom line is that partnering should be powered first by enlightened self-interest: the *total spend,* while considering commercial and technical complexity relative to business impact and supply market challenges (Figure 5.7).

---

### OPERATIONAL INNOVATION: STRATEGIC SOURCING

**Solectron Corp.,** the world's second largest electronics contract manufacturer, faced serious time-to-market issues. In response, the company changed its purchasing protocol by dividing its purchasing group into two units: strategic and tactical. Within its strategic group, Solectron established two major focal points. One group focuses on customer-specific global supply chain issues for major customers, whereas the other focuses on commodities, such as memory, passives, and interconnect devices, on a global level. Solectron's revenues increased from $400 million in 1992 to approximately $2.8 billion in 1996.*

*James Carbone, "Solectron Focuses on Strategic Buying," *Purchasing,* 121, no. 7 (7 November 1996): 79(2).

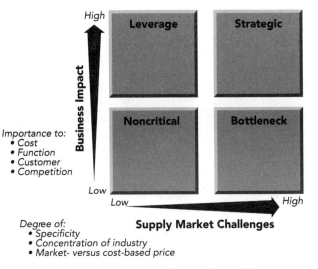

**Figure 5.7** Supply and spend portfolio.

In general, most companies should engage in relatively few, highly collaborative relationships: the kinds in which the mutual risks and rewards are significant enough to define corporate performance. In fact, there tend to be fewer collaborative relationships in sourcing and supplier management than in most other business processes. Traditional, open-market, negotiated interactions—for example, with companies supplying commodity products—should continue to represent the bulk of sourcing relationships.

The remaining few partnerships, however, will require a good deal of a sourcing organization's attention, because these relationships have to be *really managed*. They likely represent a small percentage of the supplier base, but they may still demand as much as 80 percent of a staff's time, because they often yield as much as 80 percent or more of the dollars. In net, 2 to 3 percent of total supply chain relationships is probably a good target for maximum collaboration in most organizations.

Finally, it is important to remember that strategic partnerships are not a panacea. They are difficult to execute.

---

### OPERATIONAL INNOVATION: COMMODITY TEAMS

**Donnelly,** a manufacturer of automotive interior and exterior mirrors, interior lighting systems, and interior trim, has global, cross-functional commodity teams. The commodity teams consist of representatives from purchasing, supplier quality assurance, advanced engineering, and program management. Supplier consolidation, target-pricing techniques, multiyear productivity agreements, annual purchases, and structured buy reviews are some of the strategies shared among the commodity teams. Significant purchasing cost savings have resulted.*

*Kevin R. Fitzgerald, "Automakers' Strategies Must Change at the First Tier," *Purchasing,* 121, no. 9 (12 December 1996): 65(2).

---

Objectives and operating criteria frequently conflict. Also, cooperation can be maintained only as long as there is mutual competitive advantage to be derived. Business literature is full of stories about prominent companies that have successful supplier and sourcing partnerships—the tip of the iceberg. Less often publicized are the bulk of such efforts that fail because they have not been identified, set up, and managed intelligently. Equally important, some suppliers can easily (and may even intend to) become competitors. Thus, buyers need to develop and validate alternative sources of supply as part of their ongoing operations and sourcing contingency plans.

## ■ SUMMARY: TRANSFORMING SOURCING

Strategic sourcing can reduce the total cost of externally purchased materials, goods, and services, while maintaining high levels of quality, service, and technology (Figure 5.8). An effective, efficient, and adaptable sourcing and supplier-

## OPERATIONAL INNOVATION: BECOMING A WORLD-CLASS CUSTOMER

**Black and Decker**'s stated goal is to be "a world-class customer." George Hupfer, Vice President of Global Sourcing for the North American Power Tools Division stated, "World-class customers have the inherent advantage of a supplier base that works with them."

management approach is based on total life cycle costs, cycle time, quality, and risk management. That approach also embodies the company's best assessment of its own core and key competencies, as well as those of its suppliers. Most importantly, strategic sourcing tracks to specific, well-

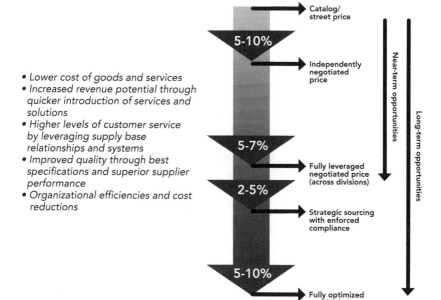

**Figure 5.8** Companies using good sourcing and supplier-management practices can realize unique benefits.

---

### ASK YOUR MANAGERS

1. What is your strategy for partnerships and/or alliances? Does it fit with the portfolio concept?

2. What programs or initiatives are under way to change the ways in which materials and supplies are bought?

3. Has your organization tried commodity teams, supplier councils, or key supplier account representatives to improve sourcing productivity?

4. What opportunities exist to reduce the company's number of suppliers?

5. Have you investigated the different uses of information technology (e.g., electronic procurement or procurement cards)? How much might they save our company?

6. Has the sourcing organization found a proper blend of centralization/decentralization?

---

communicated business goals. When all these things happen in concert, good things happen to the organization—like a (typical) 3- to 10-percent hike in the bottom line. In addition to increased profitability, executives can look for:

➤ Reduced product time to market

➤ Higher adherence to target cost/functionality

➤ Consistent purchase price reduction per year

➤ Reduced inventory levels/quality problems

➤ Improved factory/delivery performance

➤ Lower asset levels because of a core competence focus

➤ Greater contributions from the extended enterprise

In the final analysis, companies with outstanding sourcing performance emphasize the bottom line. Most have obtained executive commitment to building the organization's sourcing capabilities and have implemented a number, if not all, of the ten strategies laid out earlier. These organizations relentlessly deploy and measure these capabilities across the business and as a result, they work with a unique, world-class, and global supply base.

## ■ ENDNOTE

[1]Conducted by Ernst & Young, the University of Virginia's Darden Graduate School of Business, and the University of Western Ontario's Ivey School of Business.

# The New Logistics: Moving Less ... Faster!

Every year, more activities gather beneath the supply chain umbrella. From farm-to-pantry and silicon to scrap, all sorts of business functions and processes are joining the chain. But in the rush to new concepts and structures, supply chain basics like moving and stocking are often overlooked. These distribution and transportation functions used to be considered mission critical, and though they are still essential (as well as the largest cost buckets in the supply chain after raw materials are purchased), many companies believe that efficiency efforts have tapped all the value they have to offer.

However, geographical and physical separation of places and people still exist. Products still have to be moved from one point to another. Companies still must deploy (or stock) inventory, and every sourcing or sales decision has upstream and downstream distribution implications. Therefore, the ability of distribution and transportation to enhance enterprise value should still be acknowledged—not necessarily at the truckload, pallet, container, or unit-loading device level, but at the *strategic value level*. Explaining the role of moving and stocking in a supply chain that is enterprise-market-value focused—and introducing some new ways to move less ... faster—are the very themes of this chapter.

> *"Basic transportation and distribution functions are the largest activity cost buckets in the supply chain. International shippers spend about 7 percent of total sales on transport."*

With multiple geographies, time zones, physical space, and points of interface, global logistics is inherently complicated. Figure 6.1 demonstrates how this complexity relates to a typical consumer good (say, footwear or apparel) that is produced in one part of the world and sold at retail in another. The point is that even with the best systems, the best supply chain strategy and processes, and the best technology, tangible goods still must be moved and stocked. Companies that perform these necessary functions exceptionally well are, in multiple ways, adding genuine value to their business operations.

## ■ THE NEW VALUE OF DISTRIBUTION AND TRANSPORTATION MANAGEMENT

A variety of trends highlight distribution and transportation management's potential to *enhance value*. Among the most

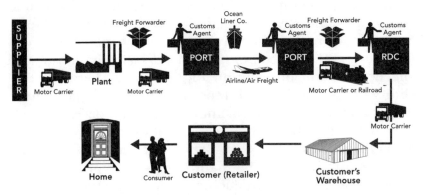

**Figure 6.1** In a typical global supply chain, a consumer product may be handled by as many as 12 different organizations.

impactful is *channel proliferation.* New delivery mechanisms appear regularly, many in response to competitive or market pressures that emphasize service. In the grocery industry, for example, more than half of all consumer purchases now bypass the grocery retailer; alternative channels such as fast food, home delivery, and office canteens have elevated distribution and transportation's role as a value-generation tool. In addition, direct distribution channels are emerging as a result of innovations in communications technology. Information enablement increases the power of traditional distribution channels in industries such as financial services, entertainment, and publishing. This also drives a higher level of complexity in the supply chain; for example, delivering to a retailer's central distribution center is much less complex than delivering to that retailer's individual stores. The net effect is that channel proliferation inspires smart companies to make excellence in moving and storing a point of differentiation (Figure 6.2).

*Greater geographical coverage*—globality—also changes the role and impact of distribution and transportation. This is

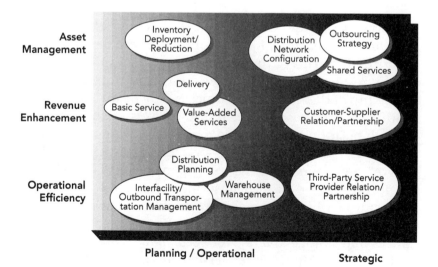

**Figure 6.2** Excellence in distribution and transportation adds value at all levels.

because more and more companies' material and component sources, manufacturing operations, and target markets are international. Consider Europe, where competitive advantages are accruing to companies that rationalized their supply chains post-1992. North Americans have fewer concerns about language, currency, culture, service standards, and technology, but the point is still valid. NAFTA, for example, has changed the cost structure for many companies' sourcing, manufacturing, and transportation activities. And in emerging markets throughout Asia and Latin America, distribution and transportation basics are essential to sales. There and elsewhere, early adapters that are first to differentiate on these dimensions are typically the most successful in keeping customers. In fact, on most continents, companies that have made decisive make-and-move responses to a geographically diverse market are often rewarded with sustainable competitive advantage.

---

*"Channel proliferation inspires smart companies to make excellence in moving and storing a point of differentiation."*

---

Perhaps the highest profile influencer is the *changing relationship of push and pull.* More and more customers are dictating the terms of their service relationship with suppliers. In response, suppliers feel compelled to take greater ownership of the transaction process. The result is deliberate stratification of customers: multiple levels of service based on each customer's economic or strategic value to the supplier. High-quality, pull-based service is typically called for with "A" customers, whereas less expensive push service may be appropriate for most "B" customers. For many companies, the result is a hybrid system in which the market differentiators are storage and delivery *excellence* in some circumstances and storage and delivery *economy* in others.

Together, these trends tell us that *effective* distribution and transportation operations must transcend operational *efficiency.* More than ever—because they improve supply chain asset management and help to increase revenues—distribution and transportation are vital tools for actualizing and enhancing business strategies.

## ■ IMPROVING THE DEPLOYMENT AND MANAGEMENT OF ASSETS

By managing assets better, companies enhance value in two ways. First, they reduce capital expenditures. Distribution and transportation skills help companies do this by rationalizing distribution networks, leveraging outsourcing opportunities, sharing services and facilities, and improving the tax effectiveness of supply chain management. The second way is by making reductions in working capital. Exceptional performance in moving and stocking helps companies reduce working capital by cutting inventories through warehouse consolidation, replacing inventory with information, reducing distribution cycle time, and implementing demand-driven planning (Figure 6.3).

### ➤ 1. Rationalize Distribution Networks

More and more companies are becoming international marketers and sellers. In addition to expanding markets, this globalization exposes new ways for businesses to organize their production and distribution facilities. Two key enablers explain why this is true:

> ➤ *Government trade liberalization* (e.g., EEC, NAFTA) has scaled back border controls, created a more homogeneous business environment (including standardization in monetary policies and accounting and tax rules), harmonized information transmission and management standards, and deregulated transportation.

---

### To Improve Deployment and Management of Assets...

---

#### Reduce Capital Expenditures by Improving Usage of Fixed Assets

1. Rationalize distribution networks.
2. Outsource select processes.
3. Explore shared facilities.
4. Use transportation and distribution equipment optimally.
5. Understand supply chain tax implications.

#### Reduce Working Capital by Minimizing Inventories

6. Consolidate warehouses.
7. Use in-transit warehousing.
8. Replace inventories with information.
9. Reduce distribution cycle time.
10. Implement demand/supply planning and management.

---

**Figure 6.3** Improving value through better asset management.

➤ *Improvements in infrastructure* have fueled growth in three areas. International distribution service providers have benefited from better road and rail transport. Improved telecommunications infrastructure has created more and tighter business relationships, even in developing countries. Lastly, information technology developments, such as regional/global enterprise resource planning systems, have altered performance benchmarks and distribution economics.

Because of these events, companies have greater freedom to build regional or global operations networks that more closely reflect their desired mix of service excellence and cost management. More than ever, their focus can be on how to best (and most economically) serve the totality of their markets, whether it is with a greater number of focused plants, fewer facilities to achieve economies of scale, or even shared-plant capacity.

> *"The complete supply chain must be optimized far more intensively than in the past."*

Obviously, these are difficult trade-offs. Fewer plants and lower production costs, for example, may be offset by higher transportation costs, longer lead times, less flexibility, and stiffer inventory requirements. The biggest challenge, however, is that the *complete supply chain* must be optimized far more intensively than in the past. This is because more is expected of it. Demand that cannot be forecasted accurately must be answered very quickly. The mantra is *quick information upstream and quick delivery downstream.* If one or both are not consistently possible, then the only alternative is padded inventories. That's the biggest trade-off.

> *"The mantra is* quick information upstream and quick delivery downstream. *If one or both are not consistently possible, then the only alternative is padded inventories."*

To make solid trade-off decisions, every company must have a high-level, logistics decision maker who understands how to rationalize distribution networks. Senior executives, on the other hand, need to understand the value potential of their companies' distribution network, as well as the opportunities that network rationalization offers. They can start by demanding answers to a key set of questions:

➤ Given that customer service drives network design, what are the service requirements for each customer category by product and channel? Relative to cost and asset utilization, how well are these requirements being met?

➤ What additional service and cost benefits could be derived from a rationalized distribution network configuration?

> ## OPERATIONAL INNOVATION: LOGISTICS ALLIANCES
>
> **Saturn, Xerox, and Whirlpool** use third-party logistics companies to leverage logistics as a competitive weapon and focus their businesses more tightly on what they do best. Like many other large manufacturers, they have recognized the important role third-party logistics companies can play in managing the supply chains of other shippers.*
>
> *Thomas A. Foster, "Leading the Way in Logistics Outsourcing," *Distribution*, 95, no. 11 (October 1996): 48–50.

➤ What would that optimal network configuration look like? How might its business benefits stack up against its implementation costs (ROI)?

➤ What is the effectiveness gap between current and optimal network configuration? What impact would a migration to a higher-performance network have on existing distribution operations?

➤ What form would a high-level implementation plan need to take?

Finally, it is important to recognize that there is no single, predefined way to rationalize distribution network operations. Nor is there a set pattern based on product groupings, even though product standardization levels (e.g., global versus regional) greatly impact network rationalization potential. Figure 6.4 depicts examples of alternative network strategies.

Despite a multiplicity of approaches, guidelines do exist for achieving value through distribution network rationalization. They include evaluating the network frequently (many companies do so quarterly or even monthly); applying sophisticated computer-based tools (models); and determining ways to become more flexible about opening, closing,

| Supply Chain Strategy | Formula Common to All Markets | Packaging Common to All Markets | Possible Supply Chain Responses | Potential Benefits |
|---|---|---|---|---|
| Total product line strategy | Yes | Yes | **Centralized Operations:** Fully centralized production and distribution | Economies of scale in production and distribution |
| | No | Yes | **Bundled Manufacturing:** Design product for customization at latest stages of production | Rationalization of components simplifies inbound logistics and improves quality |
| | No | No | **Deferred Finishing:** Final configuration of product at market | Rationalization of components simplifies inbound logistics and improves quality |
| | Yes | No | **Deferred Packing:** Labeling and packing at market warehouse | Economies of scale in production; less inventory with better customer service |
| Differentiated product strategy | No | No | **Limited:** Little opportunity for logistics reconfiguration | Economies of scale in production; less inventory with better customer service |

**Figure 6.4** Examples of alternative network strategies.

changing, or expanding stocking points. This last guideline raises one final question that each business executive must ask: "Why do we own distribution assets at all? Unless our returns on assets greatly exceed the value of flexibility, maybe we should replace distribution assets with something else."

## AN IN-DEPTH ANALYSIS OF COST/SERVICE TRADE-OFFS

**To determine the optimum distribution network configuration,** supply chain managers need to undertake an in-depth analysis of cost/service trade-offs. This entails finding the answers to questions such as:

➤ Which customers should be served by each warehouse or plant, with what products, and in what quantities?

➤ Which warehouses must be served by each plant/supplier with which products, in what quantities? Should any be dedicated to specific customers, products, channels, or geographies?

➤ How will changes in demand affect the proposed configuration?

➤ How many distribution facilities and plants are required?

➤ Where should each facility be located?

➤ How much inventory is required at each facility (by product type) to ensure a given level of order completeness?

➤ Which combination of transportation modes should be used?

➤ What is the best mix of transportation services for moving product through the network?

## ➤ 2. Outsource Select Processes

Core competencies are all the rage. Companies everywhere are being told to revisit their basic business mission and to deify only those skills and specialties that contribute directly to that mission. To ensure profitability and market differentiation, noncore processes should be outsourced.

In most contexts this is good advice. Leading toy companies, for example, excel on the basis of how well they sell toys—not how well they do accounts payable. Also, outsourcing does allow companies to focus more of their resources and time on the things that they do best (their core competencies) and that create the most value. But the line between core and noncore processes is getting blurrier. Every day, for example, more products become generic while logistical efficiencies result in lower prices. As a result, more service categories become market differentiators. So, as the key determinant of service, into which category do supply chain functions fall?

At first glance, it seems that service *is* becoming such a significant differentiator that enabling processes such as distribution and transportation should be core. More and more companies are taking this view. They recognize that their logistics processes can add genuine value and, thus, warrant the status of an internal profit center. Many have implemented sophisticated charge-back mechanisms and improved cost monitoring to support this position. Some have even molded themselves into external profit centers that market their expertise to external customers. In this capacity, in-house departments have (ironically) become third-party providers.

Maintaining and elevating an in-house logistics process has worked for a variety of companies; however, it is vital that the decision never be made purely on the basis of how core the company considers its supply chain functions. One

## OPERATIONAL INNOVATION: LOGISTICS ALLIANCES

**Allied-Signal Engineered Materials** has reengineered its transportation and logistics operations to better serve the company's global markets. The company's transportation and logistics department is now centralized, with long-term partnering relationships established with preferred carriers.*

*Ken Cottrill, "Intermodal Shipping at the Crossroads," *Journal of Business Strategy*, 18, no. 3 (May 1997): 30–5.

reason is that there will always be certain advantages offered by third parties that internal resources would be hard pressed or ill advised to match. For example, outsource relationships allow companies to:

➤ Avoid large fixed capital investments or working capital consumptions.

➤ Reduce net supply chain costs by leveraging third-party providers' economies of scale.

➤ Penetrate (or experiment with) new markets more quickly and with less capital.

➤ Leverage specialized skills and technologies that cannot be justified in-house.

The best third-party providers understand the strategic importance of supply chain management, and they are positioning themselves to provide more and better services that overcome their clients' concerns about relinquishing control of a key (if not core) competency. Today, most providers offer a range of services that complement the specific needs and capabilities of their clients. The general trend, however, is for third parties to function as full-service providers, thus ensuring that all services desired by clients can be supplied at least as completely and cost effectively outside the organization as within (Figure 6.5).

Most senior executives directly influence the key outsourcing decisions made by their companies. But on an ongoing basis, they must also be attuned to subtle shifts in business goals, market trends, and customer relationships in a way that department heads—the ones managing the outsourcing relationships—are not. Thus, it is the senior executive's responsibility to solicit information about the ongoing compatibility of outsource arrangements with long-range business goals and strategies. Put another way, outsource relationships are partnerships that thrive on complementary capabilities and long-term commitments. How are these characteristics affected by

| Classical Outsourcing | Advanced Services | Full Service |
|---|---|---|
| ➤ Warehouse management | ➤ Pick and pack | ➤ Order processing |
| | ➤ Assembly/ packaging | ➤ Order planning |
| ➤ Transportation | ➤ Returns | ➤ Systems/IT |
| ➤ Dispatch | ➤ Labeling | ➤ Invoicing |
| ➤ Delivery documentation | Price | ➤ Payment collection |
| | Bar code | ➤ Logistics consulting |
| ➤ Custom documentation | ➤ Stock count | ➤ Shipment tracking |
| | | ➤ Materials planning |

**Figure 6.5** Third-party logistics providers offer an increasingly broad range of services.

a push toward globalization? How will relationships change in light of increasingly demand-driven operations? How will service levels and bottom lines survive the supply chain responses to these trends? How can these events be predicted?

Some of these questions are answered more easily than others. For example, increasingly global operations require proven global partners, not global promises. And because flexibility requires deep technology resources, it may be less complex to quantify a prospective partner's ability to respond to a more demanding marketplace. Lastly, outsource partners must be joint problem solvers and providers of intelligence about the marketplace. *Insight* is one of many products that savvy companies must seek in a prospective outsource provider.

The impact of solid outsourcing choices can be significant—often 25 percent of total logistics costs. It is even possible to link outsource decisions to business changes using the measures discussed in Chapters 2 and 5. However, many companies have lost revenues and market opportunities by making bad decisions about what to outsource or not to outsource, choosing the wrong provider, or staying with a provider whose capabilities no longer complement the company's business objectives. Thus, it is incumbent on the executive to demand regular input on outsourcing opportunities and existing relationships. As conditions, markets, and capabilities change, the opportunities, risks, and benefits associated with outsourcing will change as well.

---

*"Intelligence about the marketplace is one of many products that savvy companies must seek in a prospective outsource provider."*

---

A key message for business executives is, whereas outsourcing selected processes is increasingly valuable, you cannot outsource management. The best outsourcing relationships exist as partnerships, not as subcontracts or task orders. The supply chain is too important to be managed by anyone who is not an integral member of the extended enterprise.

## ➤ 3. Explore Shared Facilities

In recent years, many companies rationalized their back-office functions by centralizing activities like transaction processing and payroll. In Europe, for example, multiple national and regional organizations often use one financial services center. This same principle of shared services also works well in the supply chain. In order management, customer service, purchasing, and distribution operations, considerable savings in fixed assets and operational costs are achievable.

Clearly, it is tricky to share (and thus centralize) customer-facing processes, particularly in Europe with its cultural and linguistic eclecticism and the tug of national/geographic marketing and sales organizations. However, for many processes (usually those with low levels of customer intervention), sharing/centralizing can be an attractive proposition. Even for certain customer-facing activities, such as phone-based order placement, technology is making

## MAXIMIZING THE STRATEGIC POTENTIAL OF OUTSOURCING

Today, a growing number of large companies have chosen to put (at least some of) their key logistics processes in the hands of third-party providers. However, not all outsourcing of moving and storing processes has been successful, much less, strategic. For example, although most arrangements have reduced unit costs (e.g., the cost to ship a product) or at least kept them from increasing disproportionately, few of those arrangements have actually improved customer service appreciably. Primarily, this is because service-level agreements tend to be inflexible, even as business conditions change. Moreover, any third-party service company must—like its clients—maintain operating margins.

This inability to effect *strategic* outsourcing improvements is leading to a change in how business leaders view logistics outsourcing. A concept of *joint ventures* is now emerging, whereby an outsource-minded company sets up its logistics experts in a new company, alongside outside experts that supply additional strengths in areas such as process management and systems. This outsourcing/joint venture exists solely to manage logistics activities for the one company. Its key benefits are fundamentally more strategic. They include open-book operations, profit or gain sharing, multiple opportunities for differentiation, and dedicated resources that are flexible in services, yet committed in focus. Although early innovators will experience some risk, the payoffs for being first in one's industry can be substantial and imminently sustainable.

shared services work. For example, computerized item configuration, price calculation, and available-to-promise functionality make it possible to centralize order management functions using fewer staff that are less expert and, thereby, less costly. In general terms, shared supply chain activities should be transparent. As long as comparable (or improved) delivery performance is achieved, customers won't care about what's going on in the background.

How can senior executives know if the shared service concept is viable for their companies? In the case of shared distribution *services,* they first need to determine if sufficient synergies exist in their distribution activities. No real benefits result from centralizing nonduplicated or completely dissimilar activities; likewise, if distribution activities are highly division specific, centralization will add little value. Sometimes, however, there is merit to establishing a mix of central and local activities (e.g., a central advisory logistics and contracting service with continued local operations).

In the case of shared distribution *facilities,* the greatest potential for cost savings and service improvement exists when multiple distribution facilities serve the same customers, channels, or geographic areas. If there are no obvious overlaps, cost savings may still be attainable by moving to larger centralized warehousing facilities to achieve economies of scale, reap the benefits of increased automation, or capture opportunities to balance demand on the service delivery system (e.g., by capitalizing on a product's seasonality). In either event, executives must determine whether facilities should be shared at a national, regional, or even global level.

Obviously, shared services are the basis of outsourcing: distribution volume from multiple companies is pooled to gain advantages of scale. However, companies with overlapping customers, distribution requirements, or channels can likewise share an in-house distribution function. Such horizontally shared services are more leading edge (as well as capital-intensive), but they are happening. In the pharmaceutical industry, for instance, four companies (the "Pharma 4") jointly own one distribution center. Multiple pharmacies and hospitals within a geographic market are also sharing storage facilities. In Europe, environmental concerns are behind the development of Citylogistics, whereby deliveries from a range of manufacturers are bundled outside metropolitan areas by a service provider that then brings them to retailers.

## ➤ 4. Use Transportation and Distribution Equipment Optimally

Many companies own (or lease) private vehicles or other equipment to meet special needs, for example, making plant-to-plant runs or accommodating customer-specific delivery requirements. Likewise, third-party logistics providers that use outside parties or contract carriers to move and store goods will still have a lot of their own equipment. In these and other cases, it is important that such equipment be acquired and deployed in a rational manner, that is, with the goal of reaching maximum profitability through innovative, stratified service. There are several areas in which better capital equipment optimization can add particular value:

➤ *Intermodal transport.* Increased use of two or more transport modes, typically highway (road) and rail, can dramatically improve the equipment-utilization profiles of many companies. Such containerization and "piggyback" operations have long been a logistical staple in the United States, whereas intermodal service in Europe and the rest of the world has caught on more slowly.

➤ *Global positioning satellites.* Space satellites can track and route transport equipment with pinpoint accuracy. Working in tandem with computer models, positioning satellites add value by helping to ensure that each piece of equipment is optimally positioned.

➤ *Cross docking.* Cross docking simply means unloading large loads at one end of a warehouse or DC, and moving their components directly to multiple staging/loading areas for delivery to customers (Figure 6.6). In this context, cross docking stretches the value of distribution centers by keeping goods in motion. High-speed, flow-through approaches are a powerful weapon for reducing inventories, leveraging infrastructure, and improving service.

➤ *Warehouse management.* Today's trend is toward fewer, larger warehouses and distribution centers with greater

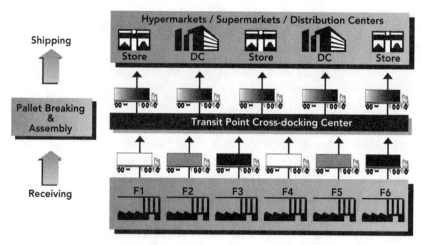

**Figure 6.6** Common cross-docking scheme.

capacity for value-added services such as product repackaging, labeling configuration, or customizing. Warehouse management systems now include radio frequency equipment, advanced picking systems, productivity enhancing technology, and automatic identification. All these technologies are geared toward the optimal use of facilities and labor.

## ➤ 5. Improve Asset Deployment through Tax-Effective Supply Chain Management

At most large companies, national boundaries often separate key operations such as manufacturing and procurement. Today, however, the international business environment is more homogeneous than ever, and companies are working hard to identify panregional, and even global, supply chain synergies. A far deeper understanding of taxation and transfer pricing must accompany these efforts.

Traditionally, companies created an integrated supply chain structure based on the physical flow of product and the digital flow of information. Working within this already-conceived structure, their tax people then tried to develop transfer prices and taxes.

Today, companies cannot omit tax and transfer-pricing issues from their *initial* structural planning activities. With today's emphasis on global rationalization, strategies into which tax and transfer issues are factored will not look the same as those that make tax and transfer pricing part of the initial planning process. Value-optimized supply chains, in other words, require tax-effective structures that are consistent with basic business requirements (Figure 6.7). This strategic alignment may be lost when tax and transfer-pricing concerns are treated as strategic retrofits.

Tax and transfer-pricing considerations are heavily affected by moving, stocking, and final configuration of products. Crossing national borders incurs customs duties, business taxes, value-added taxes, and other financial obligations. For many companies, these impositions often cost more than the raw materials used to make the product. That is why business executives must insist on full costing analyses that factor tax implications into their choice of facility location alternatives, transport options, and supply chain routings.

Even companies that have implemented tax-efficient distribution and operations structures may benefit from new net-

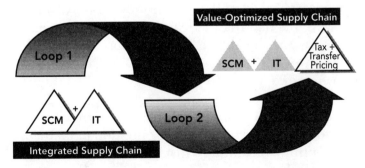

**Figure 6.7** Tax and transfer pricing distinguish the value-optimized supply chain from the integrated supply chain.

work strategies and configurations. For instance, supply chain gains (e.g., through lower costs or improved service) may be more valuable than a beneficial tax structure. Again, the pharmaceuticals industry is a good example: because of intense government intervention, a doubly keen knowledge of the trade-offs between tax and transfer-pricing structures and supply chain efficiency is critical. Our experiences show that jointly optimizing supply chains and worldwide taxes can result in up to 87 percent more improvement potential than by working on them separately. For a typical, multinational company, this could mean up to $100 million in free cash flow (after-tax dollars) alone.

## ➤ 6. Reduce Inventory through Warehouse Consolidation

The long-term benefits of a wholly reengineered supply chain are much greater than what is achievable solely through warehouse consolidation. So, however, are the risks and capital outlays. This is why warehouse consolidation programs are an attractive precursor to more sweeping supply chain initiatives.

Consolidating inventories by reducing warehouse space is conceptually simple: reduce the number of warehouses, and inventory levels will fall commensurately. More difficult, however, is making the leap from inventory reductions to cost savings. After all, fewer warehouses result in longer distances from customers, which, in turn, create transportation, service, and/or staffing penalties.

This single trade-off is surprisingly complex. To make it work, executives must focus on scope; that is, they must decide whether to rationalize through consolidation or take a broader view and optimize customer satisfaction and costs by rationalizing several components of the integrated network (e.g., manufacturing processes and locations or distribution channels and locations). Warehouse utilization analyses should also be performed regularly to respond to changing strategies, markets, products, and competitors. In other words, they must ask: "How are our warehouse operations *adding value?*" All too often, utilization is defined as labor productivity and not as value-adding processes such as final assembly, packaging, labeling, or postponement activities. This must change.

## ➤ 7. Use In-Transit Warehousing

FedEx refers to its goods-movement services as "warehouses in the sky." Like more and more companies, it understands that goods in motion are "inventory," and that they possess much of the same rationalization potential as goods that are "at rest" in a stocking location or warehouse. With this broad perspective, innovative managers have found several approaches to gaining value. Three of the most significant include:

> ➤ *Merge in transit.* Largely created by Dell Computer and its key partners, this method represents the ultimate

---

**OPERATIONAL INNOVATION: CONTINUOUS REPLENISHMENT**

**Campbell Soup Company** is in an industry that—because of stable, predictable demand and long life cycles—yields low profit margins. To extend margins, the company is working to increase the inventory turns of participating retailers by implementing a continuous replenishment program via EDI. Thus far, Campbell has successfully cut the inventories of four participating retailers from about four weeks' supply to two. This was achieved by reducing delivery lead times and making inventory levels of all retailers more visible.*

*Marshall L. Fisher, "What Is the Right Supply Chain for Your Product?," *Harvard Business Review* (19 March 1997).

in materials management postponement: merging different components (some stocked at a merge-in-transit hub and others made and shipped to order) en route to a customer's delivery site is one of the bases of build-to-order capability.

➤ *Tracking and tracing.* "Total pipeline visibility" for all shipments—regardless of where they are and in whose control—can be a powerful strategic advantage. Such knowledge allows managers not only to control their in-transit inventories, but also to divert product to higher-priority destinations such as a plant that suddenly needs a key part or a customer with a critical product need. Sophisticated automatic identification systems and technologies, and global positioning and tracking technologies, together with new information systems and improved processes, soon will result in complete supply chain visibility on a global basis. Tracing at the individual part or item level also will be available, which will further revolutionize global supply chain management.

➤ *Data warehousing.* New information technologies permit the accumulation and use of jumbo databases for in-transit inventory management. For example, data

---

### OPERATIONAL INNOVATION: CONTINUOUS REPLENISHMENT

**Procter & Gamble**'s continuous replenishment program enables the company to communicate electronically (via EDI) with customers such as Wal-Mart. This, in turn, makes it possible to quickly replenish lean retailer shelves, because P&G is notified as soon as each SKU is pulled out of the system. Since implementing CR, **Wal-Mart** has had increased inventory turns and reduced administrative costs, while P&G is enjoying 30 percent greater order volumes and a 4-percent increase in market share."*

*J. P. Donlon, "Maximizing Value in the Supply Chain," *Chief Executive*, no. 117 (October 1996): 54–63.

warehouses are under development that contain worldwide tariffs, customs information, tax rules, shipping schedules, flight plans, costs, transit times, and all other information needed to plan and control moves.

➤ *Trade finance.* New and innovative financing methods are being introduced by leading global banks, often in collaboration with global logistics service providers. Letters of credit and other financing mechanisms influence cash flow significantly around in-transit inventories, and this financing of inventories provides flexibility in terms of deploying inventory.

## ➤ 8. Leveraging Information to Reduce Inventories

Effective inventory management programs minimize stocking levels without harming service levels. At many companies, however, inventory management processes are inefficient because:

➤ Singular, unambiguous responsibility for inventory levels does not exist.

➤ The relationship between inventory and customer service levels is not well understood: inventory is maintained "just in case," additional spares and returns are largely hidden from executive view.

➤ Products are continuously added but seldom phased out.

➤ Excess or obsolete inventory is not disposed of in a timely manner.

➤ Inventory is not managed or deployed across the entire supply chain in a comprehensive manner.

➤ Information about supply chain inventories is insufficient, unavailable, or inappropriately presented. Worse yet, it is often inaccurate and untimely.

This last problem is the most ubiquitous and the most harmful. No company can efficiently manage inventory without business systems to provide vital information. After all, inventory is a buffer against uncertainty. The right information reduces uncertainty by increasing the visibility of inventory at every stocking location, as well as in transport. Hence, data accuracy, integrity, and ownership programs are a vital part of supply chain management. The right systems make it possible to identify the effective minimum inventory levels for each network location and to establish policies for maintaining and changing stock levels and managing flow between locations.

Senior executives need to know how well their existing (or planned) systems contribute to low stocking levels and desired availability levels. They need to ask:

➤ Do we have the right inventory profile and replenishment levels in every stocking location to fulfill demand (raw materials, work in process, finished goods)?

➤ Can we determine from what location every order should be fulfilled in the most effective and efficient way?

➤ What is our real-time, total pipeline inventory (raw materials, work-in-process, and finished goods inventory) at every stocking location?

➤ What is the product demand (and, thus, the distribution requirements) for each customer and group of customers served by a network location?

➤ What is the level of customer service performance (e.g., orders filled on time and complete, backorder, and stockout occurrences)?

➤ How much capital is tied up in inventory?

In recent years, the inventory-asset management capabilities of commercially available systems have increased substantially. Enterprise resource-planning (ERP) systems now provide enterprise-wide inventory information for on-line transactions. Often coupled with ERP systems are powerful new decision support systems from a variety of vendors. These tools make it possible to balance demand and supply more effectively than ever before. Inventory savings of up to 50 percent can be achieved.

The value proposition for implementing a supply chain management system is often substantial. For companies with functionally and geographically integrated business systems (and available and accurate standardized supply chain data), implementation and payback periods should be in terms of months.

To reduce inventory assets effectively, companies need to look at creative, cost-effective, and focused technology approaches, rather than going for the obvious *me-too* solution. For example, there are many viable alternatives to the relatively expensive, soup-to-nuts systems needed by companies with large supply chain-planning departments (e.g., consumer goods). These tools are more pragmatic, have richer functionality and proven interfaces with a range of disparate software and hardware architectures, and are applicable both to national and global planning processes.

## OPERATIONAL INNOVATION: INVENTORY REDUCTION

One of **Motorola**'s key supply chain objectives has been to manage activities across company boundaries in a coordinated, integrated fashion. Toward this end, the company reengineered manufacturing processes in 40 locations around the world in 20 months. The end result was improved quality, a 50 percent reduction in cycle times, and a $1 billion reduction in structural overhead. *

*Lisa H. Harrington, "Logistics, Agent for Change: Shaping the Integrated Supply Chain," *Transportation and Distribution*, 36, no. 1 (January 1995): 30–4.

## ➤ 9. Reducing Inventories by Cutting Distribution Cycle Time

Sharing information enhances the integration, sequencing, and synchronization of supply chain activities. When everyone "reads from the same page," suppliers, manufacturers, wholesalers, retailers, and third-party service providers cut costs, reduce inventories, and improve decision making.

One program that has been particularly potent at leveraging information to increase supply chain effectiveness is continuous replenishment (CRP)—a partnership between manufacturer(s) and retailer(s)/wholesaler(s), whose mutual goal is to quickly and economically replenish the retailer's/wholesaler's warehouse. Continuous replenishment is a stark contrast to traditional replenishment models, in which manufacturers push inventory into distributors' warehouses in response to forward buys, and retailers eventually pull out portions of that inventory to meet customer demand. Because there is no synchronization between these operations, administrative inefficiencies, inflated manufacturing costs, and excess inventory-carrying costs are unavoidable.

Continuous replenishment synchronizes push and pull replenishment activities. Correctly implemented, it:

➤ Reduces total pipeline inventory by eliminating unnecessary buffer stocks

➤ Accelerates overall product flow throughout the supply chain

➤ Lessens the cost of carrying inventory by reducing safety stocks, increasing channel turns, and eliminating slow moving and obsolete items

➤ Minimizes and simplifies warehousing requirements by reducing the need for interim storage (e.g., through cross-docking, merge in transit, and merge at customer dock)

➤ Increases sales by improving service performance (e.g., through better assortments and availability)

Continuous replenishment began its life in the grocery industry as a component of efficient consumer response (ECR). But in reality, it offers potential benefits to any complex, multitiered supply chain. Therefore, it is incumbent on business executives in industries such as medical products/healthcare, automotive parts supply, and wholesale distribution to understand the potential relevance of CRP to their businesses. They should ask, for example:

➤ What are our competitors doing? Do we want to be the industry pioneer? Do we have a choice?

➤ Can we find a partner with which to share risks and benefits? Would this partner need to account for a large portion of revenue?

➤ What broad operational and cultural changes might be required to make CRP work?

➤ What level of systems investment is required, and what alternatives exist in CRP software?

➤ What level of sophistication would be required? For example, should replenishment decisions be based on timely POS data or warehouse withdrawal data? Can CRP be implemented one program at a time, or is it necessary to go for scale volumes to justify program costs?

➤ From what sources can broad-brush cost-benefit and risk analyses be obtained?

➤ What opportunities do we have to observe (and learn from) other companies' experiences?

## ➤ 10. Implementing Demand-Driven Planning

Demand/supply planning, as discussed in Chapter 3, is especially relevant to making and stocking because of its significant impact on finished goods inventories. In fact, a company's ability to transform its operating strategies and methods from make-to-stock (or forecast) to make-to-actual-demand (or order) is among the greatest determinants of a company's ability to move less—faster.

However, making the transition (i.e., integrating pull and push planning) is far more complex than simply implementing demand management software systems. In reality, demand-driven logistics requires changes in strategy, process, performance, customer relationships, and even organizational principles and behavior.

Using many of the demand-planning concepts outlined in this book, a number of leading companies have achieved substantial gains in asset deployment and management. Some of these achievements (attained by well-known companies over four years) include:

➤ Increased finished goods inventory turns from 8 to 80

➤ Reduced working capital from 25 percent of sales to 6 percent

➤ Attained zero inventory in certain selected channels (sell one, make one)

➤ Eliminated asset deployment, handling, and middlemen, saving 30 percent in costs and 50 percent in time

With their demand/supply-planning mechanisms integrated with basic moving and stocking operations, the asset-management contributions of these companies' logistics operations have increased significantly.

## ■ INCREASING REVENUES

Leading companies know that satisfying customers better than the competition usually leads to revenue or sales growth. All other things being equal, customers will buy from suppliers that are easy to deal with, that deliver what they promise, and that find ways to add value to their business performance.

In other words, increasing customer satisfaction is key to increasing revenues.

Distribution and transportation have a direct impact on customer satisfaction. On-time delivery is the most obvious example—the more a supplier delivers product when the customer wants it, the more likely the customer is to continue doing business with that supplier.

However, the heat is on to offer customers added value at multiple points on the supply chain. And because they can reduce global logistics costs and streamline operations and deliveries, transportation and distribution expertise is a significant source of value. The key to harnessing that value is successfully surmounting the logistical challenges that are inherent in global supply chains: cultural differences, customs clearances, currency differences, and deficiencies in the infrastructure and technology of the world's fastest growing markets, to name a few. The earlier discussions about improving the deployment and management of assets must be evaluated not only for cost-reduction potential but also for increasing revenues. Figure 6.8 shows the various asset clusters in delivering through multiple channels. It also asks the question, "Can we be virtual and still be competitive or gain an advantage over competitors?"

As noted earlier, delivery excellence is only one revenue-enhancement measure. All told, there are dozens (e.g., quality, price, service). But harnessing them (and, thus, raising revenues) requires a new supply chain perspective: a change in how business leaders view the customer fulfillment process, organize their partners, and innovate their distribution and transportation operations within each fulfillment channel.

All of these improvements orbit a single tenet: *don't manage the supply chain on a material-flow basis.* This is because optimal material flow relies on an almost unattainable requirement—consistently perfect handoffs at numerous intersections. The reality, unfortunately, is that every intersect point is an opportunity for money to slip through,

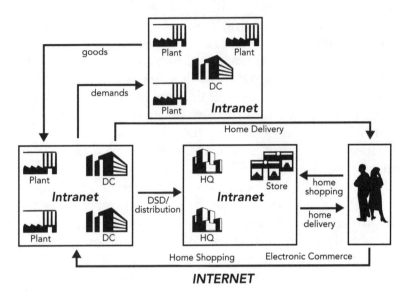

**Figure 6.8** Virtual supply chain logistics.

information to slip through, costs to increase, and customer service to degrade.

Companies seeking higher revenues through distribution and transportation need an alternative to this classical method. One way is to focus on supply chain structures and management approaches that increase the visibility of value and reduce handoff opportunities in which the ball typically gets dropped. This means order fulfillment processes based on customer segment and channel, rather than on material flowthrough. As noted in Chapter 2, this implies a multiprocess value-added fulfill process, a service/repair fulfill process, a direct flowthrough fulfill process, and a retail fulfill process (Figure 6.9).

Unlike the classical depiction, this fulfillment model is not a single supply chain or a single demand-management chain. Rather, it is two or three interlocking processes, each of which may be controlled by different companies, customers, retailers, manufacturers, and suppliers. The key point is that

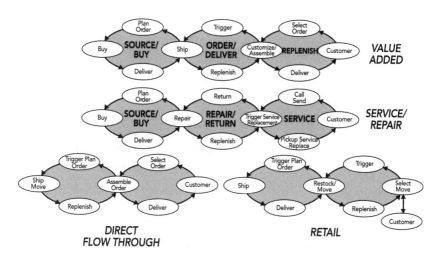

**Figure 6.9** Order fulfillment approaches by channel.

these activities are not one integrated process. Each has different goals, markings, targets, and market dynamics that make complete integration difficult, especially in the absence of strong collaborative partnerships. Five keys exist for making this model work:

1. *Segment by customer and by channel* according to profit/margin goals and strategic intent. Manufacturers must be able to meet the most stringent customer service requirements; however, they should use that capability selectively (e.g., when it is a competitive imperative or when the action satisfies a particular strategy). This can only be attained if key capabilities and resources are focused on certain high-margin and high-potential segments and channels. Service levels should be managed and differentiated by channel and segment. The point is: Do what's necessary to be competitive and meet customer expectations—but don't try to be the best in everything. The mantra is *no unnecessary excellence.*

2. *Ensure that as little product as possible sits still.* Figure 6.10 shows the relationship between service and margins in the classic customer service curve. The higher the service level, the greater the cost. However, segmenting service by channels or customers produces different margin points and higher margin potential overall. Now by *managing velocity* (the speed and direction of the product), companies don't change the shape of the curve so much as *move* it (Figure 6.11). Improving velocity can result in a higher level of customer service and/or lower cost. This can be a formidable advantage over competitors that continue to manage customer levels to cost.

---

*"No unnecessary excellence."*

---

3. *Focus on the handoffs.* Problems of all kinds congregate along the fault lines of different functions, entities, and supply chains: communication breakdowns, slipups in ownership (responsibility), inventory and material buildup, quality drops, and process ineffi-

---

## OPERATIONAL INNOVATION: INVENTORY REDUCTION

**Spartan Stores** is a $2 billion wholesaler that distributes to 474 independent supermarkets in the Midwest. To develop an efficient pull system based on consumer demand, Spartan did away with forward buying. In partnership with **Procter & Gamble,** Spartan succeeded in reducing P&G on-hand inventory from $65 million to $45 million, increasing product turns from 12 to 18, and raising its percentage of perfect orders (delivered on time, complete, damage free, with accurate billing) from 65 to 82 percent.*

*Gary Robins, "Sailing into ECR's Uncharted Waters," *Stores,* 76, no. 10 (October 1994): 43–4.

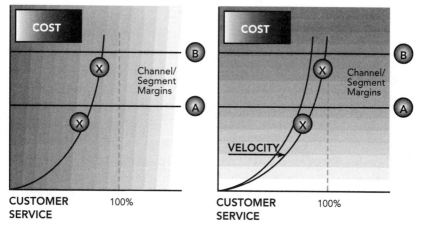

**Figure 6.10** Classical customer service curve.

**Figure 6.11** Impact of managing velocity.

ciencies. Value-focused efforts must reduce handoff requirements and improve the management of the handoffs that remain. These are achieved through demand/supply management, information exchange and linkage, and collaborative partnerships.

> "Focus on the handoffs from one department to another and from one company to another."

4. *Become information managers.* Information must replace assets for the fulfillment process to contribute greater and more quantifiable value. In supply chain management, information systems add consistency and linkage and limit redundancy among external relationships, interprocess handoffs, and geographic regions. They are the cornerstone of cost-saving postponement initiatives and—through better decision support—the key to strategic sourcing and lower inventories. Finally, technology helps to ensure the

measurement of each process's contribution to market value, share price, and profit.

5. *Simplify*. Focus on simplifying product lines, customer sets, physical assets, and the fulfillment processes themselves. Rewards include improved capability, capacity, flexibility, consistency, and cost superiority.

Armed with these strategies, business leaders can achieve higher levels of customer satisfaction—and, thus, increased revenues—through better moving and stocking. Some of these innovations may come through new transportation capabilities, such as those mentioned earlier:

➤ Airfreight advances in cost, scope, scale, handling, and storage
➤ Dynamic routing and scheduling tools
➤ Time-definite delivery services by third parties
➤ In-transit merges
➤ Intermodal services
➤ Containerization improvements
➤ Cross-docking
➤ Land-sea-air bridges

Others will emanate from advanced inventory management methods, such as:

➤ Global shipment/SKU tracking and tracing
➤ Automatic counting
➤ Mobile inventories
➤ Global positioning satellites

Advanced technologies like these are becoming more available as companies and logistics service providers strive for better customer service and lower unit cost. The ongoing supply chain challenge is to choose the specific set of methods that satisfies your markets at a reasonable cost but without unnecessary service excellence or expense.

## ■ MAKING CHANGE

Moving and stocking are the most basic of logistics processes. Yet neither is particularly well understood by business executives—especially in the context of creating competitive advantage. The reality, however, is that moving and stocking acumen heavily influences three critical success measures: time, cost, and accuracy. Visible benefits to customers—cycle time, speed, reliability in deliveries, and information value—can elevate satisfaction levels, customer value, and, therefore, sales.

> *"Moving and stocking acumen heavily influences three critical success measures: time, cost, and accuracy."*

In one sense, the most fundamental change needed to create value is one of *perspective:* philosophically recasting necessary costs as competitive leverage points. The mandate for executives is not to understand the complexities of distribution and transportation—only to recognize that, in addition to operational efficiency, these functions have taken on significant responsibility for asset management and revenue enhancement. Competence in the basics of moving and stocking is important to customers and to the bottom lines of the companies that serve them.

## ASK YOUR MANAGERS

1. What *value*, if any, does your company place on moving and stocking (transportation and distribution)? Are these functions viewed as cost centers only, or are there valuation mechanisms for service and, thus, value to customers?

2. Do your asset management strategy and practices include attention to working capital? Fixed capital? Are logistics assets (e.g., inventory, facilities, equipment) managed for *returns* or for cost/expenses?

3. Do you outsource any logistics functions? If so, are you satisfied? If not, why not? How do/would you make such a decision?

4. Do you consider taxes when planning and/or managing your supply chains? Are these choices evaluated simultaneously or independently? Do your managers understand why they are so interrelated?

5. Do your managers consider innovations in transportation and/or distribution when your profitable growth goals are addressed (for example, merge-in-transit)? Would your company spend more on moving and stocking to gain higher customer satisfaction?

6. Do you consider your company's logistics capabilities to be typical or exceptional? Why don't your logistics managers suggest ways to move less . . . faster?

# Improving the Odds: New Product Introductions and the Supply Chain

Developing, introducing, and supporting new products is one of the most challenging and vital processes that a company can undertake. One reason is that new product introductions, like the supply chain itself, traverse the entire organization. Exceptionally high levels of communication, coordination, and multifunctional planning are needed to ensure product and supply availability, manufacturability, serviceability, deliverability, and a host of other criteria essential for success. This chapter focuses on one important aspect of the new product introduction cycle: the successful *operationalization* of new products.

Operationalizing new products refers to how a company identifies, marshals, and organizes the resources needed to make new products happen and keep them happening—in other words, how the parts get sourced and acquired, how they get built, how they are stored and delivered, and what planning processes are needed to support them throughout their life and replacement cycles. It's basically supply chain management for new products: the basic activities that support focused, new product functions, such as conceptualizing, designing, prototyping, prioritizing, and introducing.

Figure 7.1 describes the classical new product development process. Often referred to as a phase review or gate process, this activity involves a series of stages, each of which is bordered by gates (go/no-go). These gates are defined by the business contract. This is typically developed at the preconcept and concept phases and specify requirements in terms of sales projections, target costs, margins, production/logistics impacts, and time. The most common problem with the classical approach actually has more to do with execution than design: operations tends to get involved too late, typically after the product has been developed. As a result, the process's key activities often happen *to* a company's operational and supply chain functions, rather than working in lockstep with a coordinated supply chain effort. For example:

➤ Manufacturing, supplier, manufacturing technology, and materials requirements are provided too late in the

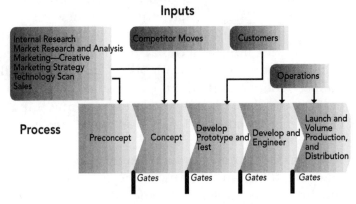

**Figure 7.1** The classical new product development process. Note the weight given to design engineering and the late involvement of operations in the process and detailed planning.

## WHAT ARE THE ODDS: ONE IN THREE?

A common myth is that 90+ percent of new products fail; the reality, however, may not be nearly so pessimistic. According to a July 1997 report in *Progressive Grocer* (supported by E&Y), traditional new product success measurements often don't account for regionally targeted or micromarket-oriented products.

In the grocery products industry, a new product is considered a success if it achieves at least 80 percent of 26-week sales per distributing store after two years. "Of all the new products reviewed, 33 percent had volume equal to or greater than they had when they were introduced; 42 percent were still in distribution but suffering declining volume; and 25 percent had failed or been discontinued. When line extensions were measured, 28 percent were seen as successes by the study criteria; 44 percent were still in distribution but suffering declines; and 28 percent had failed. 'New brands' had a significantly higher success rate: 47 percent of all new brands had succeeded; 35 percent were still in distribution but declining; and only 18 percent were considered actual failures."*

*Ryan Mathews, "Shattering the Myths," *Progressive Grocer* (July 1997): 11.

process to have any significant impact on product design and specification.

➤ Suppliers are specified, exclusive of any sourcing strategy, function, or approved supplier list.

➤ Physical and functional specifications are created, independent of operational capabilities.

➤ Cost reduction programs are developed after new product introduction and in lieu of setting up-front target costs and managing them.

➤ A product's components and parts are designed without examining their compatibility or commonality with existing parts, components, or designs.

➤ End-of-product-life conditions and considerations are analyzed and specified only when a new product or technology generation is in the market.

➤ End-of-service-life considerations are rarely specified at all.

➤ Sales projections often overlook issues, such as initial ramp-ups by market geography and cannibalization of existing product sales (thus creating problems of availability, including lost sales and erratic inventory levels).

➤ Product footprints are seldom standardized for packaging, shipping, and delivery.

➤ The assumption is often made that processes and practices from one industry are wholly applicable to others and that all products go through a common process, whether they need to be on a fast track or not.

The net effect is that new products are regularly designed and finalized without a design for operations to ensure economical and effective manufacturability, serviceability, packagability, transportability, and, most importantly, fully

---

### OPERATIONAL INNOVATION: INVENTORY AVAILABILITY DURING PRODUCT LAUNCH

**Frito-Lay's** "Baked Lay's" are the most successful new product in the history of the salted snack category and the largest-selling new item of the 1990s. However, despite a massive, day-and-night effort to ramp up production, the company's marketing successes still outstripped its ability to supply the new product to eager consumers captured by Frito-Lay's super-model ad campaign. Thus, the company was forced to juggle consumer and retail customer demand during a year-long process of building another production line.*

*Ryan Mathews, "Anatomy of a Success Story," *Progressive Grocer* (July 1997): 16.

integrated planning and execution throughout the product life cycle. This translates to a host of unfortunate consequences. If a company is lucky, perhaps those consequences will simply create a moderate case of panorganizational inconvenience. More likely, however, failing to operationalize new product introductions will lead to a much broader range of costly and potentially deadly outcomes, such as:

➤ Too many engineering changes, resulting in quality, cost, and delivery failures, as well as high frustration levels among operations personnel.

➤ Too much inventory, with the danger of rapid obsolescence (e.g., as unsold inventory rapidly crosses shelf life, stability, and technology generation time horizons).

➤ Too little inventory, leading to lost sales and margins, customer dissatisfaction, and possible customer attrition.

➤ Sourcing failures relating to quality of components, or service and availability failures relating to the supplier. This is especially common when suppliers have not been rigorously evaluated or certified.

➤ Higher material costs because of uniqueness of components and lack of commonality.

➤ Higher planning costs because of overall increased material, supplier, and component complexity.

➤ High cost of service and spares—products end up being serviced far beyond their economic life and far too many spares must be managed and deployed.

➤ High cost of packaging, when too many sizes and materials must be procured and stored.

➤ High cost of transportation, resulting from difficulties consolidating loads in a rational manner.

➤ High manufacturing costs because of unstable manufacturing processes, training, and technologies (e.g., products are released into production without adequate finalization or stabilization of the production process).

➤ Damaging delays in the market presence of competitively necessary products.

Some or most of these symptoms can be found in every new product (or product at the end of its life cycle).

---

*"Codevelopment is not the same as concurrent development."*

---

## ■ IMPROVING THE ODDS

Several practices greatly improve the odds of successfully introducing (and phasing out) new products. Those practices focus on integrating current capabilities and operational concerns with the new product development process—not merely assessing the market potential or technical feasibility of the proposed product. Remember, supply chain excellence clearly contributes to the visible differentiation that products must demonstrate to succeed in the marketplace. Thus, new product designs also include operational considerations, such as manufacturability, supply chain management, serviceability, commonality, and sustaining engineering; criteria for phaseout, replacement, end-of-product life, and end-of-service life; and parameters for customer involvement. In other words, a *design for operation*. The common threads are *collaborative work, joint problem solving,* and *planning for product life cycles*. Figure 7.2 shows an enhanced phase review process that explicitly recognizes introduction as a vital and early component. Note the integration of operations, customers, suppliers, and partners early on, as well as the detailed business contract-planning phase. This is really the key to successful new product introductions. After all, it is easy to develop new options and designs (relatively speaking), but it is much more difficult to operationalize and manage those options, especially after the fact.

## ■ OPERATIONAL TENETS FOR NEW PRODUCT DEVELOPMENT

### ➤ 1. Link Plans for New Product Phasein and Phaseout to the Enterprise-Wide Demand/ Supply Planning Process

The new product development and introduction cycle is never smooth. Schedule decommits and recommits are an

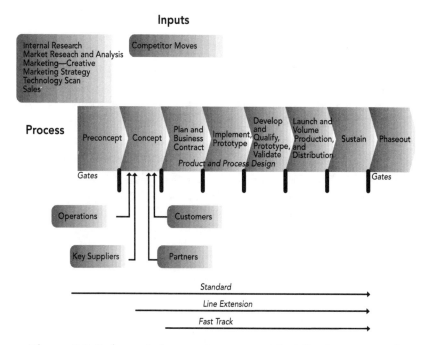

**Figure 7.2** Enhanced phase review, new product development, and introduction process. Note the early integration of operations, key suppliers, third-party partners, and customers. Note the different variants for line extension and fast-track products.

---

### OPERATIONAL INNOVATION: PLANNING FOR MANUFACTURABILITY

In 1995, **Warner-Lambert** and **Glaxo Wellcome** joined forces to bring Zantac 75 to the marketplace. Because the over-the-counter, acid-relief category was already being addressed by competitive products such as Pepcid AC and Tagamet HB, the Zantac 75 partners worked particularly hard on production forecasting. Much effort was devoted to building accurate forecasts and developing high and low production estimates. Top-down and bottom-up models were developed to help ensure accurate forecasts. To date, Zantac 75 has made a significant dent in this $8- to 10-million-per-week market.*

*Ryan Mathews, "Making the Switch," *Progressive Grocer* (July 1997): 20.

---

inherent part of the process. Nevertheless, demand/supply management must incorporate new product plans—from introduction through phaseout—at the earliest stages of the process. Not doing this will hurt a company's control of costs and product availability, and it will damage the cooperative strategies that may already have been implemented by manufacturing, marketing, logistics, and sales. Moreover, early involvement is crucial, because unique demand/supply imperatives exist at each phase in the new product development life cycle. For example:

➤ *During introduction and evaluation:* Low product and component volumes drive the need for early delivery of parts and components. Higher unit costs may result at this stage. Planning should be done separately for engineering components, which have a different set of costs, manufacturing standards, and procurement criteria.

➤ *During ramp-up:* High product availability is crucial. Some increase in relative inventory levels is acceptable.

➤ *As the product matures:* Needs shift to tight inventory deployment and management of spares. Bill-of-material-specified inventory, high procurement efficiencies, and lower-cost material replacements are necessary to maximize customer service for key segments and maintain low, system-wide carrying costs.

➤ *During phaseout:* Attention turns to replacement inventories (to take up demand slack) and low inventories (to avoid excess and obsolete stocks). This is when new products are phased in, and inventory must be tightly managed to ensure that overall levels do not rise.

➤ *At end of product life:* Inventory focus is on spares until end-of-service life is reached. After that, emphasis is on replacements (sometimes including lifetime buys). Remember, however, that lifetime buys are a purchasing solution, not a business or financial solution. Sometimes it is more cost effective to provide a new unit than it is to stock spares for an older, obsolete unit or product generation.

## ➤ 2. Create Product and Operations Processes Simultaneously

Not many companies integrate the product design and operational processes. Even fewer do it effectively. Nevertheless, this linkage is one of the most important tenets of new product development (designing for operations). However, this does not mean *concurrent* development. It is *codevelopment—* the integration of product, processes, supply base, channel requirements, and technology. The difference is significant. Only codevelopment ensures that new or changed processes are jointly developed, tested, stabilized, and documented *before* ramp-up and volume production. Thus, it minimizes the likelihood of interruptions because of design concerns.

The goal is to get to market as early as possible in an economical fashion with the right volumes of quality, stable products.

---

*"The business contract must be a sales, finance, design, engineering, and operations document."*

---

Virtually all parts of the supply chain must be addressed to mount a successful, integrated, codevelopment effort:

➤ *Procurement and supplier management.* Global activities include developing and maintaining approved supplier lists (certified as technical, capacity, process, quality, flexibility, and delivery capability); evaluating new suppliers; understanding the available industry supply and capacity base (as well as new process and material technologies being developed); ensuring component and material commonality; and quantifying cost impacts and trends.

➤ *Production.* New product development and operations personnel must understand and coordinate production process capabilities, extensions, and possibilities; new production technologies; and outsource/copacking capacities and capabilities. A key element is stabilizing the process and training the workforce before the product hits the volume production/ramp-up stage.

➤ *Distribution.* Codevelopment strategies and tactics must be developed for getting the product to the right customers, at the right place, and at the right time. Consideration should be given to packaging options, existing configurations, storage ease, packing and palletization, and footprint to allow for maximum delivery efficiency. Replenishment programs, reverse logistics, and logistical support for returns and repair must also be addressed. Finally, it is important to incorporate design criteria that are geared toward display and takedown for those products that must be deployed on shelves or at trade shows.

---

**OPERATIONAL INNOVATION: CROSS-FUNCTIONAL TEAMS**

**Eastman Kodak**'s development of the one-time-use camera represented a significant departure from the company's traditional "inside-to-outside" product development approach. Instead of basing new product development on (internal) technological innovations, the company turned to the marketplace and developed Voice of the Retailer (VOR) and Voice of the Consumer (VOC) new product programs. Key to the success of these programs were cross-functional teams, comprising manufacturing, design, marketing, and research and development. With maximum input from inside and outside the company, Kodak's Fun Saver Pocket cameras now garner some $500 million in sales per year.*

*Ryan Mathews, "The Voice of the Consumer," *Progressive Grocer* (July 1997): 26.

---

➤ *Demand/supply management.* As discussed earlier, a coordinated approach must be developed for addressing analogs for demand planning; handling inventory deployment across multiple product sets and life cycles; and managing commits, decommits, and recommits in the demand/supply plan.

➤ *Service.* Issues here include serviceability ease and options, creation of field-replaceable units and replacement policies (in particular, at the end of product life), field diagnostics, and cost trade-offs for maximizing customer service satisfaction and cost efficiency. This would include the entire returns process, including repair.

Figure 7.3 overviews the above activities and explains their supply chain impacts. As can be seen, codevelopment is very high impact. In fact, it often represents the difference between new product success and product profitability, and introduction failure and cost disadvantage.

| Codevelopment Action | Business Goal | Supply Chain Impact |
| --- | --- | --- |
| Develop and maintain supplier lists (certified) | Ensure product quality, consistency of delivery, flexibility in reacting to demand changes, and technical process capability to handle product specifications, reduce costs over time, and produce new-generation products. | ▲ Quality<br>▲ Flexibility<br>▼ Costs |
| Evaluate new suppliers | Ensure alignment of supplier base with company needs. | ▲ Quality |
| Understand available industry and capacity base | Plan for adequate supply capacity and contingencies in case of supply disruption. | ▲ Flexibility |
| Maximize component and material commonality | Reduce and manage numbers of unique parts and leverage component commonality for reduced costs, inventory management, and interchangeability among product lines. | ▼ Costs |
| Coordinate production process capabilities, technologies, and possibilities. Train workforce. | Ensure smooth transition from engineering production to volume production with as few disruptions, waste, scrap, and quality problems as possible. | ▼ Costs<br>▲ Volume<br>▲ Quality<br>▼ Waste/Rework |
| Explore outsourcing: contract manufacturing and copacking | Plan for contingencies and demand changes and minimize overall production losses per unit. | ▲ Flexibility<br>▼ Costs<br>▲ Capacity |
| Design for distribution | Ensure maximum efficiencies in packaging, transportation, and warehousing storage and shipping. | ▼ Costs |

**Figure 7.3** Codevelopment actions and their supply chain impacts.

| Codevelopment Action | Business Goal | Supply Chain Impact |
|---|---|---|
| Design replenishment programs and promotions | Plan for adequate storage and joint deliveries of promotional items, as well as storage and transportation capacities for promotional programs. | ▲ Availability<br>▼ Costs<br>▲ Flexibility |
| Implement demand/supply management and inventory deployment, including phase-in/phaseout and end-of-service life | Ensure availability and optimum total inventory levels, given the product life cycle and technology cycle stages of the product portfolio. | ▲ Service<br>▼ Costs |
| Design for serviceability | Work towards reducing *total* spares inventory and managing spares planning with minimum number of discrete items planned. | ▼ Costs |
| Analyze cost-service trade-offs | Explicitly target customer service levels and costs to serve, given the customer base segmentation. | ▲ Service<br>▼ Costs |

**Figure 7.3** *(Continued)*.

## ➤ 3. Design New Products with Maximum Parts Commonality

Focusing on commonality can significantly cut costs, minimize time requirements, and reduce complexity. Every new part, component, supplier, or process-specific specification is likely to add costs, increase breakage potential, delay introduction, and complicate justification procedures. Adhering to commonality guidelines requires disciplined processes, appropriate metrics, good information systems, and good part-numbering systems (e.g., coding and classification systems). Commonality metrics should address all aspects of the product/service bundle: parts and compo-

## OPERATIONAL INNOVATION: CROSS-COMPANY PRODUCT DEVELOPMENT

Developers at **K2** have teamed up with **Active Control Experts, Inc.**, to produce a "Smart Ski" that detects and dampens shocks and vibrations in the path of the skier. Piezoelectric and ceramic materials are embedded in the body of the laminated KT Four Smart Ski, which is intended to perform well in all snow and ice conditions. Future applications of the smart piezoelectric technology include shape control in aircraft wings, precision machinery, automobile ride comfort, and some biomedical applications.*

*Steven Ashley, "Smart Skis and Other Adaptive Structures," *Mechanical Engineering*, 117, no. 11 (November 1995): 76–81.

nents, packaging configurations, production tooling, distribution, and logistics, using providers and suppliers from the company's existing, approved supplier list (or as few *new* suppliers as possible). Figure 7.4 illustrates the impact on operations that results from a lack of commonality.

Platforms should be adopted that permit effective postponement and mass customization, the key to which is commonality. The further downstream that products can have common parts and processes, the greater the flexibility in tailoring the final product to individual customers' tastes. And the lower the overall variety of parts or components, the easier it is to design processes and make products to a near-finalized stage. In other words, commonality is a key enabler to postponement and mass customization. The most effective mass customizers design commonality into their products.

### ➤ 4. Build a Better Business Contract

The business contract is probably the most important element of the new product development process. It is a com-

| What Problems Does a Lack of Commonality Cause? | Supply Chain Impact |
|---|---|
| Increases the number of parts to plan for, buy, deploy, phase in, phase out, track, and control | ➤ Overhead |
| Increases the risk of excess and obsolete inventory | ➤ Inventory |
| Increases the risk of quality problems and confusion in production | ➤ Quality<br>➤ Costs |
| Reduces leverage in purchasing, leading to higher costs per unit | ➤ Procurement costs |
| Reduces throughput because of increased changeovers and setups, and cycle time through rework | ➤ Production costs |
| Increases design time and costs | ➤ Time (market share loss)<br>➤ Design costs |
| Increases risk of poor design integration | ➤ Engineering change control costs |
| Increases service complexity | ➤ Service costs<br>➤ Customer service |

**Figure 7.4** The impact of insufficient commonality ripples throughout the supply chain.

prehensive business case and action plan that articulates new product development goals and targets, and describes and schedules the personnel, processes, and activities needed to reach those goals.

Developed by the product manager (or program manager) and the new product development team (which must include operations), the business contract incorporates business, customer, and competitive requirements; technology options and trends; and current manufacturing, logistics, supply, and technical capabilities. More specifically, it addresses:

➤ Cost targets at different stages of the product life cycle for development and production (rather than after-the-fact, cost reduction programs).

➤ Realistic revenue targets and margins.

➤ Commonality targets.

➤ Time targets for various phases of the development/introduction cycle, including time to market.

➤ Design quality, including postlaunch engineering change notices, quality, and reliability.

➤ Product specifications at a fairly finalized level. Product specifications should be defined as far as possible at the concept stage.

➤ Resources and team composition.

➤ The position in the product and technology portfolio.

The business contract undergoes refinement until it is frozen at the plan and prototype stages. At this point, it becomes a performance contract between the product team and senior management, with goals defined by the target metrics it contains.

> *"Although the process is important, the person who leads it is even more so."*

Given its high level of importance, the business contract must be approved by senior management and the leaders of all functional groups involved. The approval metrics used by these parties must be the individual and cumulative effects of each stage in the development/introduction cycle, even when

| OPERATIONAL INNOVATION: INVENTORY AVAILABILITY DURING PRODUCT LAUNCH |

**Microsoft**—in preparation for its release of Windows 95—constructed the most massive inventory buildup in computer industry history. On August 24, 1995 (the official product launch date), Microsoft had around five million copies in stores. Key contributors to the successful buildup were Microsoft's JIT manufacturing system, a contract network of disk duplicators, and eleven strategically placed Windows 95 warehouses.[*,†,‡]

[*]John Longwell and Tim Grace, "A Tale of Products and Pallets," *Computer Reseller News*, no. 644 (August 1995): 1, 155.

[†]Jeff Berg, "Exploring New Vistas," *Mortgage Banking*, 57, no. 1 (October 1996): 147–54.

[‡]Tim Ouellette, "As Consumers Seek Solace via On-Line Forums," *Computerworld*, 29, no. 36 (4 September 1995): 6.

the products are line extensions or replacements. Firm targets for development and volume production should be set early in the business contract process, with performance measured against these. Significant gaps can then be detected in the process, and quick action can be taken (even cutting losses by canceling the product and diverting resources to other products, if necessary).

## ➤ 5. Develop World-Class Development and Introduction Teams

Much has been written about the organizational structure required for effective new product development. However, we feel that comparatively little attention has been paid to the people aspects, particularly the characteristics of a product

## OPERATIONAL INNOVATION: ADDRESSING PRODUCT LAUNCH AND INTRODUCTION PROBLEMS

**IBM** hit on a unique and widely accepted location for the cursor-controlling device on its new Thinkpad: right in the middle of the keyboard. Unfortunately, this was a controversial design point within IBM, and focus groups had difficulty believing that it would be a hit in the marketplace. As a result, the company seriously underestimated sales of the product, resulting in shortages throughout the product's first year.*

*Marshall L. Fisher, "What Is the Right Supply Chain for Your Product?," *Harvard Business Review* (Mar/Apr 1997).

program manager and of the product development and introduction team.

Too often, a company emphasizes reporting relationships, organizational structure, and program setup, but it applies less scrutiny to its selection of a program manager. Consider that after approval of the concept, a program manager is appointed to carry the project through volume production (and sometimes to the end of the product's life cycle). This is an exceptionally important position because it encompasses responsibility for all product metrics and targets through volume ramp-up. Moreover, the position demands skills that are not always part of a typical product manager's portfolio. For example:

➤ *Excellent interpersonal skills* are needed to deal with a wide variety of upstream and downstream interests, personalities, and priorities. Similar skills are needed to communicate effectively with teams of internal, multifunctional personnel, as well as external contacts, such as suppliers, third-party partners, and customers. Program managers are also required to deal regularly with executive management to review progress, compile status information, and obtain approval through the various phase-review gates.

➤ *Multifunctional awareness* must be combined with extensive competency in a key functional area. In other words, program managers have to be generalists *and* specialists, and they must possess strong functional credibility within the organization. Program managers must be aware of the downstream and upstream *business* impacts of development decisions—particularly as they relate to operations and commonality.

➤ *Strong management skills* define the ability to direct a diverse, crossfunctional, and, at times, *cross-company* development team. In fact, different program phases require the program manager to exhibit different management skills. It may be too much, for example, to expect a technical development engineer to master volume-manufacturing methods and capabilities as the product moves towards ramp-up and introduction. This is why program managers must also be competent project managers, time managers, cost managers, performance managers, and people managers. The latter is crucial, because weeding out nonperforming team members is often required, and differing skill sets are called for over time.

Like the selection of a program manager, the team composition also requires careful thought. Some not-so-obvious characteristics of a successful, new product development/introduction team include:

➤ *Integrated and multidisciplinary from the start.* Beginning with the concept phase, program teams should include representatives from design, manufacturing, finance (particularly important), customer service, logistics, materials, procurement, sometimes marketing, and often representatives from supplier and partner compa-

> ### OPERATIONAL INNOVATION: ADDRESSING MANUFACTURABILITY AND SERVICE PROBLEMS
>
> **IBM** now includes purchasing agents in its product development process. This policy has helped solve many of the company's concerns about waiting times for parts for newly designed products. IBM's procurement development engineers report to purchasing, but they work with designers to ensure that parts designed into new IBM computers will be available. The procurement engineers maintain awareness of emerging technologies and key suppliers to develop technology roadmaps for the designers. In two years, this policy has helped IBM reduce its product development time from 12 to 15 months to 6 to 9 months.*
>
> *James Carbone, "A Buyer's Place Is in the Design Lab," *Purchasing*, 120, no. 3(3) (March 1996): 59.

nies. In a seamless fashion, knowledge should move both upstream and downstream and (if necessary) across companies. Multigeography and multicultural representation can also be crucial, particularly when products and product introductions cross national or cultural boundaries. (Don't go overboard with this one—it's only necessary some of the time.) Supply chain requirements and infrastructure are different in most countries and, therefore, must be considered carefully. Overall, the team's most important collective trait will be the ability to focus on the entire program, not just individual pieces. Studies have shown that product development/introduction teams that can do this are more effective and require significantly fewer total resources over the life of the process. To make this world view happen, companies should plan to field the *best* team, not just the best available team.

➤ *A core of full-time personnel.* Too many product development and introduction efforts fall prey to the *full-time equivalent* syndrome for key people. With this model, only the program manager and a small support staff are fully dedicated. The rest are occupationally ambivalent. The "reservist" approach does not work. Dropped balls, project delays, and cost overruns are inevitable. Fortunately, a huge, full-time complement is not needed either. What *is* required is a *multifunctional core team* that is dedicated to the product set through the sustain phase. At various program stages, additional skill sets (full time, part time, or ad hoc) can be introduced; however, continuity of the core team throughout the program is vital to successful introduction.

➤ *Colocation and a dedicated physical area.* In this era of virtuality, companies may be tempted to save space, travel time, and costs by focusing on virtual colocation. Although the active use of collaboration tools is a necessity, total reliance on them as a vehicle for joint product/process development will cause myriad problems. It is a good idea that the complete development/introduction team be *physically proximate* to ensure rapid, precise communication and an ongoing, often spontaneous, environment of information sharing. The one exception is design, which can often be handled in a remote location. However, the overall new product introduction process—production, distribution, customer service/order management, sales, and marketing—is far too complex to be managed virtually.

## ■ VALUE CHAIN JOINT DEVELOPMENT: A NEW APPROACH

A powerful new strategy for effective, new product development is rapidly finding favor with innovative companies. Value chain joint development (VCJD) is essentially a channel-specific partnering approach among manufactur-

## OPERATIONAL INNOVATION: ACCELERATING NEW PRODUCT DEVELOPMENT COLOCATION

**BMW** has cut its product development cycle by nearly two years with its creation of the largest single research engineering center in Europe. The Fiz Centre in Munich is a series of towers and connecting hallways in which nearly 6000 engineers (including first-concept designers and production line engineers) work on developing new models. To promote simultaneous engineering concepts, none of the engineers must walk more than 150 meters to talk to a colleague.*

*Delavar G. Shenas and Sepehr Derakhshan, "Organizational Approaches to the Implementation of Simultaneous Engineering," *International Journal of Operations & Production Management,* 14, no. 10: 30–43.

ers, suppliers, third parties, and customers, with strong integration among all functions in the company. It is still in the nascent stage with key aspects such as costs and profit sharing; managing line extensions and new technology generations; and priorities for development and introduction yet to be worked out. However, VCJD can be clearly a powerful mechanism for successful, targeted, product development and introduction. Several leading companies have already embraced its various components and practices.

The primary characteristics of VCJD are greater cooperation, strong integration of players throughout the supply chain, and a blurred distinction between the product introduction, ramp-up, refinement, and sales phases. Figure 7.5 illustrates the basic concepts of VCJD. The key is enterprise-wide concurrent and joint development that involves other companies (either a set venture of certain companies or different combinations of external parties and partners), and it is targeted to specific markets, uses, or channels.

Widespread use of VCJD is still some way off. Nevertheless, a number of its principles have a significant relevance

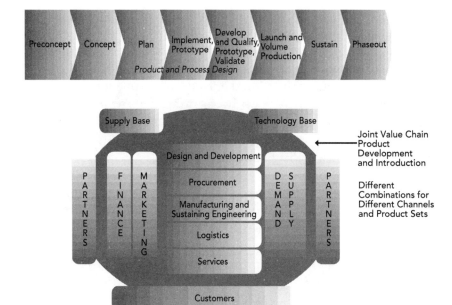

**Figure 7.5** VCJD. Joint, cross-channel product development and intro-duction targeted to a particular channel or segment is being explored by several companies.

as to how companies should approach new product develop-ment *now*. Five of these principles have been explored in this chapter. Applied together, they can dramatically improve the odds of a successful new product program.

## ■ SUMMARY

Fueling business growth in the years ahead requires the rapid and successful introduction of new products. Although the high-tech industry has learned this basic truth quite well—Dell, Compaq, Hewlett-Packard, Sun, IBM, and other PC companies are notable examples—*all industries* need new products to meet (or stimulate) customer demand. In the future, many of the world's business leaders will be those companies that do this best.

But being best in new products means more than design and development. It means integrating new products into a high-performing supply chain that, within each channel, ensures that the introduction is effective from Day One. From a supply chain perspective, therefore, new product success is a function of time, total cost, margins, and the most efficient use of working capital.

Certainly, companies can learn from other industries. Week after week, for example, the entertainment industry—compact disc makers, video manufacturers, and even the comic book trade—successfully hits retailers with new products at precisely the targeted time. The reason they do it successfully is that they *must* do it. They have to! In the future, more and more companies will *have to*. Many do now, although they may not realize it.

We have provided some good practices gleaned from our experiences with new product introductions: codevelopment, better planning, earlier and greater operational integration, and a focus on the entire process of *concept-to-end-of-life cycle*. The best companies—and those wanting to be the best—apply these practices. They work.

## ASK YOUR MANAGERS

1. What percent of your new products have problems during introduction?
2. How would they describe the new product development process? . . . the new product introduction process?
3. Are the ideas and practices discussed in this book embedded within your new product process? If not, why not?
4. How are your supply chain capabilities factored into new product development?
5. Why are the best people not on new product teams?

*Chapter* 8

# Making It Happen: The Value-Producing Supply Chain

There are three dimensions to innovating or improving the supply chain. The first dimension is the initiative's *value:* the relationship of benefits to all costs. The second is *risk* (probability of success), which is a function of the elapsed time between the start of an initiative and the moment when real, tangible benefits begin to accrue. The results of any change or innovation—whether from reengineering, systems implementation, new product or process developments, or incremental improvements—must be measured in terms of value creation versus risk. How a company approaches this challenge is represented by the third dimension: the *method* that is applied to the initiative. This chapter addresses the three key elements associated with innovating and improving the supply chain: *value, risk,* and *method.*

233

# ■ TO ENSURE VALUE

## ➤ Be Realistic about Benefits

Value (probably the most overused and abused word in the lexicon of business) can be defined as the relationship of *benefits* (immediate, ongoing, or deferred) to *all costs* (immediate, ongoing, or deferred). To get a realistic handle on that relationship, companies must avoid three pitfalls:

1. *Grossly overestimating benefits.* This is a distressingly common occurrence. So common, in fact, that one executive whom we know automatically reduces projected benefits from any proposed project by 25 percent.

2. *Grossly underestimating the time needed to obtain benefits.* That same executive automatically takes every project's proposed timeline and adds 50 percent.

3. *Overlooking the real benefits of a major supply chain initiative.* Many times, we have reviewed the justification of a major supply chain initiative and found that companies focus only on the most obvious benefits (typically, those nearest to the heart of the project champion). Conversely, they miss the more strategic benefits that really make a difference. For example, one company proposed to undertake a major effort to penetrate a new channel, justifying it with near-term sales and margin increases. What the company failed to see (and, thus, to plan for) was the strategic benefit associated with establishing a channel foothold at a time when its major competitors were dominating other, more established channels. Moreover, the company did not initially look at the high level of synergy that could be achieved between this channel and existing channels already addressed by the company.

The key is to equate *realistic* with *tangible*. The better articulated and quantified the benefits are, the more focused and measurable the initiative becomes. However, it is also important to acknowledge the existence of a quantification hierarchy: tactical initiatives/benefits can *usually* be quantified; strategic initiatives/benefits can *sometimes* be quantified; and infrastructure-related initiatives/benefits can *rarely* be quantified. Sometimes, therefore, value must be ascertained during an iterative process of honest, open dialogue between parties who represent differing perspectives, but who can be trusted to address the company's overarching interests. (If different functions have their compensations tied to the business's goals, this should pose little problem.)

### ➤ Be Very Critical about Costs

Assessing benefits is a small challenge compared to the difficult task of assessing the true costs of an initiative. True costs include *all related costs:* internal and opportunity costs, true inventory costs (particularly for new programs), contractor costs, systems costs, support costs, and, of course, the usual asset-based costs. Thus, true costs for a major supply chain initiative (particularly a global one) are often several times the obvious cost of assets, hardware, and software. And remember: value is the relationship of true benefits to *all costs.*

## ■ TO REALLY MANAGE RISK

### ➤ Remember that Short-Term Initiatives Are More Likely to Succeed than Long-Term Ones

Short-term initiatives usually have very definitive targets, action plans, and horizons; usually, they are very specific about resources required, benefits, and costs. Long-term initiatives, on the other hand, are generally hazy about true value (benefits versus costs). More often than not, project timing is underestimated and value overestimated.

## ➤ Consider that Discrete Initiatives that Tackle Parts of a Large Problem Are More Likely to Succeed than Silver Bullets

This is intuitively obvious; nevertheless, far too many companies revere the silver bullet. Large, end-to-end supply chain-reengineering projects or global, enterprise-wide, systems implementation projects are typical examples. A few of these do succeed—a few! But a much larger number achieve only a fraction of their intended (overly optimistic) benefits—usually after an uncomfortably long period of time. Finally, there are probably as many projects that crash and burn spectacularly as there are projects that succeed spectacularly. Several studies point to reengineering success rates of 20 to 50 percent. More and more practitioners and consultants, however, believe that the lower end is more accurate. All in all, reengineering the complete spectrum of supply chain activities in one seven-league step is a very risky way to generate value. A better solution is to implement in stages.

---

*"If you want to change anything, don't try to change everything."*

---

## ➤ Implement in Stages

Significantly better odds await companies that work *in stages* to build innovation into specific business processes. With this approach, each overall process design becomes a roadmap that focuses on an end point or goal that is *not fixed*. When the end point moves (as it always does), significant but incremental changes (whether process or technology) provide the necessary flexibility and speed of response to move with it. Additionally, the organization gets a taste of success reasonably quickly, which, in turn, builds confidence and momentum.

Figure 8.1 illustrates the risk-benefit relationships of phased versus giant-step approaches. The key, of course, is to move toward the left: reducing risk as much as possible without doing nothing. Occasionally, companies must take a bet-the-farm type of risk. However, these are few and far between, and well-managed companies rarely have to confront them.

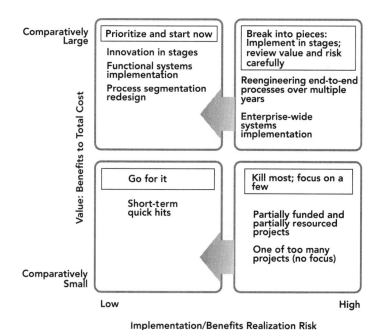

**Figure 8.1** Various approaches to innovation and improvement and their value realization potential.

## ■ TO ENSURE THE RIGHT METHOD

### ➤ First, Understand the Supply Chain

The first step toward understanding supply chain cost-benefit relationships (and developing a coherent strategy) is to map the supply chain's characteristics, material flows, stocking points, lead times, customer needs, products, and structure. The dimensions along which the supply chain must be defined and understood include:

- ➤ Mix of products (movement, costs, inventories)
- ➤ Mix of end configurations
- ➤ Products: commodity or new/innovative
- ➤ Volume per order/product (high or low)
- ➤ Volume in total (high or low)
- ➤ Product life cycle
- ➤ Service life cycle
- ➤ Commonality across product generations—parts, materials, designs
- ➤ Service response times required
- ➤ Delivery response time required
- ➤ Number of channels and the material flow
- ➤ Discrete customer segments
- ➤ Demand planning (blind forecast to collaborative planning)
- ➤ Delivery to customer from one to multiple sources
- ➤ Delivery to customer from intracompany to multiple companies

### ➤ Next, Implement a Base

The next stage is putting in place the base programs and good management practices discussed in earlier chapters: data integrity and accuracy, flexibility initiatives, enterprise-wide demand/supply management, and the operational practices needed to develop a lean supply chain. It is important to have solid supply chain operations in which the basics are executed well.

## ➤ Then, Innovate

The third stage is creating supply chain innovation—building on the operations base to restructure the supply chain globally, incorporating such elements as virtuality, segmentation, mass customization, electronic commerce, and information exchange. Figure 8.2 illustrates the progression.

## ■ THINKING, DOING, LEARNING

Redesigning the supply chain on a global basis is best accomplished in stages and by segments, such as channel, customer, and geography. It should be an iterative sequence of *think, do, learn, think again, do again,* rather than interminable planning followed by interminable design, followed by interminable implementation (Figure 8.3). The key here

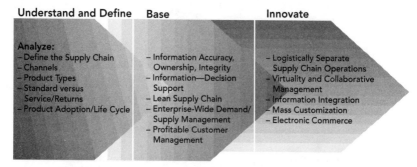

**Understand and Define**     **Base**                    **Innovate**

**Analyze:**
– Define the Supply Chain
– Channels
– Product Types
– Standard versus
   Service/Returns
– Product Adoption/Life Cycle

– Information Accuracy,
   Ownership, Integrity
– Information—Decision
   Support
– Lean Supply Chain
– Enterprise-Wide Demand/
   Supply Management
– Profitable Customer
   Management

– Logistically Separate
   Supply Chain Operations
– Virtuality and Collaborative
   Management
– Information Integration
– Mass Customization
– Electronic Commerce

**Figure 8.2** Putting it all together: the progression toward operational excellence.

is launching into action before the grand design is complete but after the supply chain is understood and specific implementation stages mapped out. Our experience has shown repeatedly that this approach will accelerate pace and size of benefits far better than silver bullets, which, in reality, never solve the problem.

The value of working in stages and by segments is best captured in a wholly counterintuitive maximum: *do less with more.* In other words, put more resources onto fewer, more implementable initiatives, and make them accountable for results. For example, one approach that practically guarantees failure is the *full-time equivalent* (FTE) approach to staffing projects. Ten FTEs could mean 100 people theoretically committing 10 percent of their work hours, with nobody actually accountable for anything (or, for that matter, *doing* anything). A second insidious approach (which is about as successful) is the *evenings-and-weekends* method. This approach assumes that people are so excited about the initiative that they are willing to devote their free time to it and not have it impinge on their day-to-day responsibilities. The point is that people must be motivated, dedicated, and accountable. *But they must also be given the time and resources to execute in a system designed to help them succeed.*

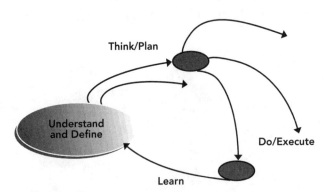

**Figure 8.3** Think, do, learn, think, do, learn: launch several smaller phases and initiatives after rapid planning, and learn from them. Don't plan and design forever.

In net, innovative responses to the fulfillment challenge are not well addressed by monolithic, global initiatives, or any other silver bullets. Almost by definition, any initiative that is too big and encompasses too many issues; that takes several years to plan, design, and implement; or that is the result of a very small group of people selecting and designing the solution set is largely guaranteed to provide disappointment and failure. What's worse, it will probably result in a great deal of wasted money and resources, a huge opportunity cost (money and talent that could have been used for new products and better processes—at the very least, they could have called on customers and accounts), and a decline in organizational credibility and morale.

An honest, real-world approach to supply chain value is to design (using a multifunctional and multigeography team) a high-level, supply chain construct that:

➤ Is based on key operational imperatives of value (costs and benefits) and risk of realizing benefits

➤ Understands the current state and dynamics of the supply chain

➤ Anticipates the changing dynamics of market and geography

➤ Builds a hedge against moving targets by following a phased implementation plan (by process segment, geography, channel, product, or customer segment)

➤ Increases the odds of success by attacking pieces with fully resourced and accountable initiatives

➤ Incorporates various initiatives as part of a value-risk portfolio

These are the keys to leveraging the global supply chain to increase EMV.

# *Appendix*

# Findings from a Study of Supply Chain Partnerships[1]

In 1997, Ernst & Young completed a landmark study as part of its Supply Chain Knowledge Partnership with the Darden Graduate School of Business Administration, and the University of Western Ontario. This study took an in-depth look at relationships across supply chains, including over 150 companies across several targeted industries around the world.

The goal was to examine these relationships across supply chains to understand the activities viewed as important by each member of the supply chain in terms of sharing learning across the supply chain, cooperation and collaboration with suppliers and customers, dealing with uncertainty, and to correlate supply chain practices to their impact on bottom-line results to identify levers of supply chain performance.

This study was the first of its kind, not only in that it looked both upstream and downstream in a single supply chain, requiring participation from both customers and suppliers, but also in that it looked at both behaviors and practices. This Appendix contains the findings from this study.

We have entered a new era in understanding the dynamics of competitive advantage and the role played by supply chain member companies. We no longer talk about suppliers and customers as though they are managed in isolation, each treated as an independent entity. More and more, we are witnessing a transformation in which suppliers and customers are inextricably linked throughout the entire sequence of events that bring materials from their source of supply, through different value-adding activities to the ultimate

243

customer. Success is no longer measured by a single transaction; competition is, in many instances, evaluated as a network of cooperating companies competing with other firms along the entire supply chain (Spekman, Salmond and Kamauff, 1994). Simply, Ford Motors is as successful as its ability to coordinate the efforts of its key suppliers (and its suppliers' suppliers) as steel, glass, plastic, and sophisticated electronic systems are transformed into an automobile that is intended to compete in world markets against the Japanese, the Germans, and other U.S. manufacturers. World-class companies are now accelerating their efforts to align processes and information flows throughout their entire value-added network to meet the rising expectations of a demanding market place. We hear from enlightened managers worldwide that success is now measured by cost, speed, innovation, and customer satisfaction.

This new view of the world advocates that the coordination of complex global networks of company activities is becoming a prime source of competitive advantage. The secret is to achieve breakthrough changes and improvements, so that the expertise of members of the value-added network is shared throughout the system. Now, we see that fill-the-order component makers are being asked to participate in the customer satisfaction delivery process as design partners, risk sharers, and engines of greater efficiency. These attempts at integrating this value-added network to achieve both customer value and competitive advantage are under the framework of supply chain management.

The study sought to understand better some of the complexities of supply chain management and to offer insights into improving the practices. Although a number of advantages accrue to firms that implement integrated supply chain practices and processes, a number of hurdles block the path. This supply chain study sheds light on problem areas across a range of relevant supply chain management processes and practices.

Most companies attempt to leverage the supply chain to achieve the lowest initial purchase prices while assuring supply. Typical characteristics include multiple partners; partner evaluations based on purchase price, cost-based information bases; arms-length negotiations; formal short-term contracts; and centralized purchasing. Operating under these conditions encourages fierce competition among suppliers, often requires playing one supplier against the others, and uses rewards or punishment based on performance.

The assumption is that trading partners are interchangeable and that they will take advantage if they become too important. In addition, there is a belief that maximum competition, under the discipline of a free market, promotes a healthy and vigorous supply base, which is predicated on the *survival of the fittest.*

Such leading companies as Boeing, Black & Decker, Hewlett Packard, and 3M are designing, developing, optimizing, and managing the internal and external components of the supply system, including material supply, transforming materials, and distributing finished products or services to customers that is consistent with overall objectives and strategies. Because each level of the supply chain focuses on a compatible set of objectives, redundant activities and duplicated effort can be reduced. In addition, supply chain partners openly share information that facilitates their ability to jointly meet end user's needs.

The new supply chain management emphasizes leveraging the skills, expertise, and capabilities of the firms who comprise this competitive network. Managers have long acknowledged the importance of getting close to their key customers. Now that this logic has extended upstream as well, it is also important to forge close ties to key suppliers. A sustainable supply chain strategy extends these linkages upstream and down. Supply chain strategy includes efforts aimed at developing and maintaining global information systems, addressing strategic aspects of make-or-buy issues, and accessing and managing innovation with the purpose of protecting and enhancing core technologies. A supply chain strategy includes sourcing strategy, information flows (internal and external), new product coordination, concurrent procurement, teaming arrangements, commodity/component strategies, long-term requirements planning, industry collaboration, and staff development.

# ■ THE NEW COMPETITION

Supply chain management extends our appreciation for the concepts of cooperation and competition. Cooperation is no longer seen as a process between one set of trading partners. Cooperation now exists along the entire supply chain. GM's Saturn division no longer cooperates with a few select parts suppliers; it finds itself partnering with many different suppliers—its inbound logistics carrier, its outbound carrier, and its retail dealer network, some of which are in Japan. They all must be synchronized to deliver product that permits Saturn to compete favorably against Toyota and Honda.

In the new competition, firms will no longer compete as they have in the past. The new competition embodies global networks of nimble firms whose managers proactively seek alternative interpretations of events, are eager to think differently about their business, and respond quickly to marketplace changes. Cooperation emphasizes the need to integrate functional silos and views these units as interdependent parts charged with meeting the end-user customer's needs. Equally important are the cooperative ties that extend to external buyers and suppliers who work together to maximize the overall effectiveness of the supply chain. What evolves is a network of interrelated firms whose primary objective is to gain strategic advantage for the whole supply chain.

The key question is how do we effectively manage and leverage the skills and talents of our supply chain partners. The procurement manager, as a broker of information rather than a transaction manager, becomes a critical participant in the process, guiding both the formation and implementation of longer-term relationships and interfirm supply networks. The purchasing professional in the new competition must add breadth while becoming, to a certain extent, a manager of external manufacturing whose responsibility spans the supply chain. He or she must use procurement-related information about products, processes, competition, and macrox/microeconomic issues that can affect the firm's competitive posture. Figure A.1 summarizes the revolutionary transformations that the new competition demands and the changes faced by the procurement manager.

# ■ FROM COOPERATION TO COLLABORATION

Within the requirements of the new competition a shift in the level of intensity among trading partners emerges. Cooperation, whereby

| Evolving Role | Revolutionary Role |
|---|---|
| Transaction accountant | Information exchange broker |
| Administers interfirm contracts | Guides the information and implementation of partnerships and interfirm networks |
| Primary point of contact with suppliers | Manager of external manufacturing |
| Interface with first-tier suppliers | Responsibilities throughout the supply chain |
| Minimizes risks (e.g., supply disruption, incoming, defects) to the buying organization | Manages and leverages the skills of the supply chain |
| Reacting to external stimuli (reactionary change) | Proactively assessing external information |
| Safeguarding proprietary/ critical information— transaction driven | Enhancing information sharing through the value chain—early supplier involvement |
| Unidirectional communications | Simultaneous two-way communication |
| Cross-functional coordination | Functional integration |
| Cause-and-effect problem solving | Systems thinking |
| Purchasing mentality | World view |

**Figure A.1** The company's intrinsic stock price versus working capital investment rate.

firms exchange bits of essential information and engage some suppliers/customers in longer-term contracts, has become the threshold level of interaction. Cooperation is the starting point for effective supply chain management and has become a necessary, but not sufficient, condition. The next level of intensity is coordination, whereby both specified workflow and information is exchanged in a manner that permits JIT systems, EDI, and other mechanisms that attempt to make seamless many of the traditional linkages between and among trading parties. Trading parties can cooperate and coordinate certain activities but still not behave as true partners.

Effective supply chain management is built on a foundation of trust and commitment. Trust is conveyed through faith, reliance, belief, or confidence in the supply partner and is viewed as a willingness to forego opportunistic behavior. Commitment is the belief that the trading partners are willing to devote energy to sustaining this relationship. Through commitment, partners dedicate resources to sustain and further the goals of the supply chain. To a large degree, commitment "ups the ante" and makes it more difficult for partners to act in ways that might adversely affect overall supply chain performance. Trading partners throughout the supply chain become integrated into their major customers' processes and more tied to their overarching goals. For instance, supply chain partners willingly share information about future plans and designs, competitive forces, and R&D. Partners recognize that their long-term success is as strong as their weakest supply chain partner. For example, Boeing competes for global market share with its engine manufacturer, its landing gear supplier, and the host of firms who supply components, expertise, and knowledge that ultimately are incorporated in the 777 or 7X7. Boeing is successful because its supply chain partners are focused on winning bids from Airbus and its set of European supply chain partners.

Figure A.2 summarizes the transition from being an important supplier to becoming a supply chain partner. The changes required to move from one level to another require changes in mind-set and strategic orientation among supply chain partners. In most instances, firms have already achieved cooperation and coordination with key segments of their suppliers and customers. Nonetheless, the movement from coordination to collaboration requires levels of trust and commitment that are beyond those typically found in both JIT and EDI relationships. For instance, firms can coordinate production and logistics activities to ensure JIT delivery but never reach that next step of integration whereby future design, product performance, and long-term strategic intentions are shared. For example, Bose and its JIT II□ partners are further along this continuum and have dedicated unique and nonfungible resources to ensure that Bose not only serves its major customers better but is also more successful than its competitors in

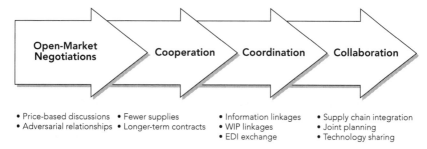

**Figure A.2** The key transition from open-market negotiations to collaboration.

world markets. We can cooperate and be coordinated in a supply chain but not collaborate. Collaboration requires high levels of trust, commitment, and information sharing among supply chain partners; in addition, partners share a common vision of the future.

Collaboration means that the tasks of the buying and selling firms are interdependent and become conduits of information between the manufacturing firm and its preferred suppliers. Collaborative buyer/seller relationships allow managers to manage these tasks better than before. Collaborative behavior engages partners in joint planning and processes beyond levels reached in less intense trading relationships. The procurement function can transcend its traditional role of contributing to "cost leadership" (which remains important but not the key driver in supply chain management), and it can support other revenue-enhancing strategic initiatives.

Effective supply chain management in the new competition seeks close, long-term, working relationships with one or two partners (both suppliers *and* customers), who depend on one another for much of their business, developing interactive relationships with partners who share information freely, work together when trying to solve common problems when designing new products, who jointly plan for the future, and who make their success interdependent. Over the long term, the supply chain that forges "virtual firm" relationships in those situations in which uncertainty is highest and in which the cost of success (or failure) is greatest will likely prevail.

# ■ THE STUDY

The purpose of this study was to examine supply chain management as it applies to developing and sustaining a competitive advantage for the firm. We investigated best practices from the perspective of the operations/procurement managers and marketing managers across a set of firms that comprise a supply chain. By focusing on buyers and sellers, we gained insight into how each viewed a range of supply chain processes and practices.

This study includes 22 aggregate supply chains from North America, South America, and Europe across five broad industry groupings (life sciences, oil and gas, consumer products, utilities, and manufacturing—high-tech electronics and automotive). An aggregate supply chain reflects the response of different levels (e.g., upstream and downstream) within the supply chain relative to a focal company. As Figure A.3 suggests, this study extends traditional studies that either asked questions of only buyers (or sellers) and only inferred information about the other trading partner, or attempted to make comparisons between trading partners. Marketers responded to questions about their internal suppliers (i.e., operations) and their external customers, while operations/procurement managers responded to questions about their external suppliers and their internal customers (i.e., marketing).[2] From these different perspectives, we are able to reflect a supply chain view of certain key dimensions of supply chain man-

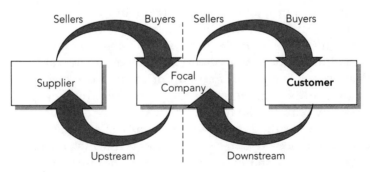

**Figure A.3** The supply chain used for the study.

agement processes and practices, as well as to show differences in perspectives across different levels of the supply chain.

# ■ THE FINDINGS

Figure A.4 reflects the ranking of information flows along the supply chain and reflects both traditional work flow metrics related to inventory, delivery, and other forms of materials tracking. In addition, the section attempts to capture those information flows that relate to customer satisfaction and the degree to which suppliers

---

### Top Ten

---

**Issue: "To what extent do you apply the following practices?"**

1. Tight linkages between customers and suppliers
2. Purchase order information tracking
3. Raw material cost, quality, and delivery tracking
4. Supplier/customer satisfaction measures
5. Finished goods visibility
6. Order entry and order-taking technology
7. Shipment tracking
8. Individual customers managed as accounts
9. Process control
10. Integrated quality information

---

### Bottom Five

---

Robotics
CAD/CAM/CAE
Flexible manufacturing cells
EDI customer links
Automatic storage and retrieval systems

---

**Figure A.4** Information flow supply chain factors.

and customers are linked. Three of the top ten items relate to tracking linkages between customers and suppliers (e.g., tight linkages between customers and suppliers, measures of satisfaction, and individual customers managed as account). Although measures of customer/supplier satisfaction scored relatively high, most of the informational considerations addressed were purchase order driven. In fact, all but one of the remaining items relate to information tied to tracking the flow of product as it moves from raw material, to work-in-process, to finished goods. Electronic data interchange (EDI) and other more sophisticated processes for linking supply chain members were used very little. A difference exists between *what managers say* and *what managers do*. We hear about the importance of the customer and the need to be market focused, but the results tend to reflect business as usual with a strong emphasis on measures that relate to more traditional purchasing or transactional focus.

Sellers, as expected, are more concerned with informational factors that reflect customer considerations. However, in each of the measures that track product flow, the buyers' scores were lower than the sellers. In particular, information tracking that converged on quality, process control, and other more sophisticated tracking mechanisms, such as EDI and CAD/CAM buyers scores were significantly lower than sellers. Thus, buyers appear to be less sensitive to information that links levels of the supply chain, in general, and are far less concerned about information that is directly linked to end customer considerations. This could imply a silo mentality, whereby the concern for customers is someone else's problem.

## ■ REASONS FOR SUPPLY CHAIN MANAGEMENT

Figure A.5 summarizes the results of this issue. The findings explain the virtues of supply chain management, ranging from increased end customer satisfaction, to gaining a strategic market position, to reduced costs and improved productivity. It is encouraging that the reasons reflect both the cost reduction and the revenue enhancement side of supply chain management. Buyers tend to focus more on the cost reduction aspects of supply chain management and view securing a reliable source of supply, reduced

| Top Ten |
| --- |

**Issue: "To what extent do the following reflect your reasons for engaging in supply chain management?"**

1. Increase end customer satisfaction
2. Improved profits
3. Secure reliable source/market for this item
4. Satisfy supplier/customer request
5. Reduce overall operating costs
6. Gain strategic market position
7. Reduce lead time
8. Price paid for item class
9. Improved productivity
10. Increase margins

| Bottom Five |
| --- |

Political
Regulations and tax implications
Environmental
Reduce product development costs
Local economy

**Figure A.5** Reasons to engage in supply chain management.

lead time, and lower costs as key drivers of supply chain management. Sellers, on the other hand, tend to highlight revenue enhancement and see profits, strategic market position, and customer satisfaction as prime drivers for supply chain management.

# ■ CRITICALITY

Central to supply chain management is the degree to which each member views the other as essential to success and recognizes that each supply chain partner is dependent on the other. Criticality is based on high recognized interdependence in which one supply chain member will not act in their own best interest to the detriment of the supply chain. Both customers and suppliers are important supply chain partners and view each one's participation and input as important. Figure A.6 shows that buyers are less likely to view the customer/supplier as irreplaceable and essential to their future business. We believe that this difference sheds insight into buyers' traditional commodity mentality—if supply chain partners are easily interchangeable and matter little in the future success of the buyers' firm, it becomes readily apparent why price paid looms as such a key differentiating factor. Certainly, to focus on price minimizes the leverage and loyalty engendered from the supply base, which ignores the contribution suppliers can make to a buyer's corporate strategy.

## ■ SUPPLY CHAIN PARTNER SELECTION

Figure A.7 summarizes what is valued when firms select a supply chain partner. Managers seek supply chain partners who are trust-

---

### Full Order

**Issue: "To what extent does this describe your relationship?"**

1. Items we provide this firm are important to our company.
2. The items we provide this customer are critical to our success.
3. The annual dollar amount of our supplies to this customer is large.
4. Compared with items we provide other customers, the dollar volume of items provided to this customer is major.
5. This customer is better than other customers.
6. This customer is essential to our future success in this business.
7. This supply chain member can be easily replaced. (R)

---

**Figure A.6** Overall supply chain relationships.

---

**Top Ten**

---

**Issue: "To what extent does this reflect your reasons for selecting a supply chain partner?"**

1. Is trustworthy
2. Has a high degree of integrity
3. Knows our business
4. Is reliable and consistent in dealing with us
5. Has a strong reputation
6. Supports the importance we give to customer service
7. Has potential synergy with us
8. Is committed to us
9. Improves our competitive market position
10. Offers us both economic benefit

---

**Bottom Five**

---

Offer tax incentives
Offers environmental advantages
Provides political advantages
Reduces engineering changes
Helps us achieve workforce cost reductions

---

**Figure A.7** Supply chain partner selection.

worthy, have integrity, and who know our business—characteristics that imply *fair dealing*. Certainly, both trust and commitment offset the risks of opportunistic behavior in which one acts in their own best interest to the detriment of their supply chain partners. Reputation, improvement in market position, and support of customer service are less important to buyers than sellers. This is consistent with buyers' implied focus on the cost reduction aspects of supply chain management. Buyers desire partners who know their business but are less concerned that partners offer both parties economic benefit. Buyers do appear to value trust, commitment, and reliability *and* also might seek economic gain at their partners' expense.

# ■ SUPPLY CHAIN MANAGEMENT PROCESSES

Supply chain management processes explore what firms *say they do* in their supply chain interactions. Firms tend to take a more long-term view and expect the relationship to last, sustaining the relationship is important, and they have plans to continue the relationship into the future. The firms also highlight communications processes as an important second theme. Communications between the partner firms is frequent and that there is a high level of contact between trading parties. Partners have faith in each other and report that they share a sense of fair play. When we look at key differences between buyers and sellers, it appears that buyers are less willing to devote extra effort to their supply chain relationships. These results are summarized in Figure A.8.

# ■ SUPPLY CHAIN PRACTICES

Although the aforementioned reports what supply chain members say they do, this section examines *what they actually do.* The difference is akin to "talking the talk and walking the walk." We often get the strong impression that information is shared openly and that the boundary between firms is quite permeable. However, our findings suggest that information sharing is less than open and that technical information is shared only when necessary. In addition, mixed signals surface about the importance of price in evaluating a partner. From Figure A.9, price is important, and there is some evidence that price is viewed as the key attribute in decisions. As expected, buyers appear to be more purchase price conscious than sellers, tend to be less willing to share information, and are less likely to see training as an obligation.

Firms often do not do what they say they do, and buyers appear to be reluctant supply chain partners. Buyers embrace collaboration less than sellers and fear the close ties that are required for integrated supply chain management.

---

### Top Ten

---

**Issue: "To what extent does the following describe your relationship with this supply chain partner?"**

1. We expect this relationship to last a long time.

2. There is continuous contact between our firm and this customer.

3. Sustaining this relationship is important.

4. Communication between our organization and this customer is frequent.

5. There is a high level of contact between our firm and this customer.

6. Frequent communication occurs between the firms.

7. We are willing to devote extra effort to this relationship.

8. We have plans to continue this relationship.

9. We share a similar sense of fair play with this customer.

10. We have faith in this customer.

---

### Bottom Five

---

We periodically evaluate the importance of our relationship with this customer.

We believe that this customer acts in its own best interest.

Risks are shared equitably between us and this customer.

Personnel from this customer are involved in our product design.

Rewards are shared equitably between us and this customer.

---

**Figure A.8** Supply chain management processes.

## ■ EFFECTS OF PERFORMANCE

We also sought to explain the extent to which different measures of performance—cost reduction and revenue enhancement (as measured by customer satisfaction)—are affected by different supply chain processes and practices. We examined the extent to which elements of coordination, collaboration, and criticality affect two different measures of supply chain management performance.

---

### Top Ten

---

**Issue: "To what extent does the following describe your relationship with this supply chain partner?"**

1. We exchange technical information with this customer when necessary.
2. In picking this customer, we focused on initial sales price (R).
3. In choosing this customer, we used criteria in addition to initial sales price.
4. When selecting this customer, our primary criteria was sales price (R).
5. When initially evaluating this customer, we made the selection decision based on measures other than sales price.
6. We willingly share technology information with this customer.
7. Customers to this customer (downstream customers) are an indispensable part of our overall value-added supply chain.
8. We examine this customer's competence using multiple criteria.
9. One area unilaterally evaluates this customer's capabilities.
10. Training this customer is important.

---

### Bottom Five

---

**Issue: "To what extent does the following describe your relationship with this supply chain partner?"**

We have a strong relationship with this customer's customers.
We provide training for this customer.
We emphasize training with this customer.
Our organization tends to make customer decisions at higher levels in the firm.
We consolidate decisions at high levels in this firm.

---

**Figure A.9** Supply chain management practices.

Traditional performance measures would reflect cost reduction, whereas a more "enlightened" view should also deem revenue-enhancing elements as very important. One measure focused on the contribution made to cost reduction and the other on the contribution made to customer satisfaction. Although both approaches place pressures on the supply base, cost reduction tends not to embody a win-win relationship, nor does it convey a recognition of the skill and expertise brought to the relationship by suppliers. Only by focusing on measures of customer satisfaction is it possible to assemble a world-class supply chain.

Our findings here are that both the sharing of information (a form of collaboration) and criticality contribute in a positive manner to cost reduction, whereas an element of coordination—order entry and tracking—negatively affects this measure of performance. First, coordination, by itself, does not ensure cost reduction. Second, elements of collaboration and criticality contribute to cost reduction and do so with greater impact than any of the key measures of coordination used in this study. Coordination is a necessary, but not sufficient, condition for buyers and sellers to achieve a state of supply chain improvement. A performance metric that focuses on elements of coordination to achieve cost reduction is very likely to result in suboptimal outcomes.

Our findings in customer satisfaction tell a similar story. Shared-order entry contributes to customer satisfaction, whereas a measure of close linkages between supplier and customer appears to have a negative impact. Sharing important information, the importance of sustaining the relationship, and the perceived value of training contribute positively to customer satisfaction. Workflow-related activities are useful but do not achieve the full benefits of an integrated supply chain and must be accompanied by a richer depth and breadth of shared information to achieve this important outcome. Both trust and commitment contribute to satisfaction. The elements of collaboration imply a willingness to share information without the concern for it being used against either trading partner and a longer-term focus to the trading relationship. Although the results for sustaining the relationship are counterintuitive, coordination cannot substitute for closer ties between trading partners. Interdependence and information sharing become key ingredients in an integrated supply chain whose goal is customer satisfaction.

# ■ CONCLUSIONS

It is apparent from these findings that business has not yet fully operationalized supply chain management. Buyers tend to be reluctant players and are far more skeptical about the benefits afforded through such close integration. Buyers weigh less favorably the benefits gained and are more likely to highlight the risks associated with heightened dependence on a smaller number of suppliers. Also, buyers think about the gains afforded by an integrated supply chain and are more easily swayed by more traditional purchasing metrics related to cost or initial purchase price. Buyers consistently view the cost-saving aspects of supply chain management as more important than the revenue-enhancing benefits. They seem to understand, on one level, the importance of customer-driven supply chains; the need to focus on core competencies; and the importance of leveraging the skills and capabilities of their suppliers. Yet this makes buyers uncomfortable, and they easily revert to their cost-driven behaviors in which suppliers are viewed as substitutable, and value is determined by negotiation. A gap exists between the goals and concerns of senior managers and the activities of the procurement function—buyers have not fully responded to the challenges of managing suppliers with the intent of gaining the full complement of skills afforded by an integrated supply chain.

Buyers and sellers do not share the same values and beliefs regarding the advantages of supply chain management. In fact, buyers and sellers have very little in common, and their world views tend not to converge. Although some differences are expected, this is not surprising that supply chain management practices are difficult to implement. At the very least, buyer and seller must have a shared perspective of the merits of such close ties within the supply chain. Thus, the challenge becomes one of forging a common view in which both sides can accomplish compatible goals. Buyers are less able to fill this leadership role, as they appear to lack both vision and commitment to the advantages of supply chain management. Without such leadership skills, buyers' firms suffer, and their potential competitive advantage is diminished.

We readily admit that not all trading relationships should be collaborative and that it is perfectly fine (if not absolutely necessary) to engage in arm's-length transactions, *provided that* such behavior is appropriate. Criticality, to a large degree, drives the partnering strategy employed. Trust and commitment do affect customers' satisfaction. To achieve a competitive advantage across the set of supply chain partners, our findings suggest:

> ➤ The road from open-market negotiations to cooperation, to coordination, and to collaboration is a long one and should not be traveled by each and every buyer-seller relationship.

> ➤ One must select both partners and supply chain strategies carefully. Coordination and collaboration are different, require different levels of trust and commitment, and often lead to different outcomes.

Information technology is an important enabler and is key to the development of an integrated supply chain. However, this information must be shared by the partners. Although there is a reluctance to share key information among partners, many of these fears subside if partners share similar values and a common vision. Information sharing heightens the alignment between partners, such that effective supply chains share learnings among partners rather than worry about knowledge expropriation. The role of the supply chain champion is to orchestrate this alignment and to ensure that the total supply chain is, in fact, better than the sum of its parts.

Adopting the concepts and tenets of supply chain management requires a new mind-set. The complete set of linkages that tie suppliers and customers throughout the value chain demands a business transformation. Managers should mitigate uncertainty and exploit opportunities through the creative use of suppliers and customers by evaluating who best supplies value and then leveraging that expertise/capability throughout the entire supply chain. This requires sharing what once might have been considered proprietary information, relinquishing control to others in the supply chain, and trusting that your supply chain partners will act in your best interest. Although information systems and technology enable and facilitate, success cannot succeed acting in isolation, and competitive success depends on the entire supply chain moving in unison, sharing similar goals and objectives.

In summary, business has yet to "crack the code." Supply chain partners still do not share a common vision or react to the same set

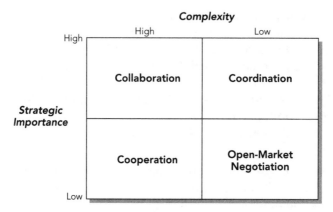

**Figure A.10** Supply chain management strategy.

of metrics. Opportunities are lost and challenges remain. For a number of firms, talk is cheap, and supply chain management is still only part of today's jargon. A number of firms are sacrificing cost effectiveness, revenue enhancement, and customer satisfaction, because they are unable to work effectively across the firms that comprise their supply chains. Figure A.10 summarizes the factors that differentiate among levels of commitment and intensity. Relationships that are both strategically important and complex to manage should be treated collaboratively. Complexity can be financial (i.e., a significant dollar commitment) or commercial (e.g., intertwined and/or interdependent technology, joint production processes, shared development). Both aspects of complexity suggest interdependence between trading partners.

Our findings are that buyers and sellers do not share a common voice and have moved slowly to bridge the gaps that separate them. Potential supply chain champions should use our findings to find synergies among supply chain partners to build tighter linkages between customers and suppliers.

# ■ ENDNOTES

[1]This Appendix is a summary of a study by Ernst & Young in 1997. A more detailed article by Robert E. Spekman, John Kamauff, and Niklas Myhr will be published on the study.

[2]The titles of these managers included both procurement and operations (i.e., manufacturing) managers. Our contacts were typically general managers who directed questionnaires to potential respondents who had working knowledge of both external suppliers *and* internal customers. During the discussion of the results, the term buyer represented data taken from either procurement *or* operation managers.

# Index

# About the Authors

**Gene Tyndall** is a Senior Partner and a leader of the Ernst & Young Global Supply Chain Practice. For more than 25 years, he has managed and implemented supply chain solutions around the world for corporations in the consumer products, high-technology, and manufacturing industries. Mr. Tyndall is also a widely published author of books, papers, and feature articles, and he is a frequent speaker/moderator at global conferences on supply chain management, operations strategy, and world trade.

**Christopher Gopal** is the U.S. National Director of Supply Chain and Operations Consulting for Ernst & Young. He is also part of the firm's Global Supply Chain Leadership Team. Before joining E&Y, Mr. Gopal was a vice president with Dell Computer Corporation. Altogether, he has more than 22 years of experience in industry, academia, and consulting; he has worked with scores of clients in strategy, supply chain management, and information technology. He has published two books, several articles, and is a frequent speaker/panel member at various forums on supply chain management and operations.

**Dr. Wolfgang Partsch** is the Managing Partner of Ernst & Young's European Supply Chain Management Consulting Practice, as well as Chairman of the firm's Global Supply Chain Network. In management consulting for more than 25 years, Dr. Partsch has managed worldwide consulting engagements in the chemicals, pharmaceuticals, electronics, and consumer products industries. He has also played a key role in the development of many innovative supply chain concepts in Europe.

**Dr. John Kamauff** is a Partner in Ernst & Young's Supply Chain/Operations Consulting Practice. Before joining E&Y, he led his own international management consulting firm. He has also taught sourcing and operations management at the Western Business School (Canada), the University of Virginia, the Koblenz School of Management in Germany, the IPADE in Mexico, and the IDE in Ecuador.